# Something To Battle With

## How to beat temptation, cut suffering and live happy

# Something To Battle With

## How to beat temptation, cut suffering and live happy

Edward Mulraine

Published in the United States by E.A. Raine Publishing, LLC

www.earainepublishing.com


Library of Congress Cataloging-in-Publication Data

Mulraine, Edward

Something to Battle With: How to beat temptation, cut suffering and live happy

ISBN: 978-0-578-14218-0

Cover Design by: Edward Mulraine, Robert Graves

FOR MORE INFORMATION ABOUT OUR TITLES, GO TO:
WWW.EARAINEPUBLISHING.COM

Something to Battle With: How to beat temptation, cut suffering and live happy

The Gathering at Gethsemane

This book is dedicated to
"You"

We must fight for the children.
Thanks to my children I am fighting.

# CONTENTS

# MY BATTLE

As I am writing this book I am also experiencing its effect. I am in retreat—fasting and praying, strengthening and cleansing my soul from internal and external depravity. I am like Henry David Thoreau, who in 1845 moved from his mother's home to a small cabin he built at Walden Pond to seek a relationship with nature and God for the purpose of solitude and liberation. Thoreau sought refuge to reflect upon his own independence from worldly affairs. He felt America had become too enmeshed in commerce, technology, industrialism, and material progress, and this public phenomenon not only overwhelmed one's home but tarnished one's soul. Thoreau at times aligned himself with groups to address the controversies of the nation; however, he sought spiritual individualism, realizing the best retreat from worldly affairs is often found in self-reflection through written discourse.

Although Thoreau retreated for two years in self-reflection and writing, I am only able to take two weeks in self-reflection and two weeks in writing upon my reflection. The reason why I am writing this book is because I am in a battle; as a matter of fact we're all in a battle—against temptation. Every living person battles against something. Whether they acknowledge it or not is their prerogative.

No one is exempt from battle. It is inevitable as well as inescapable.

And the battle is not determined by one's spiritual or secular affiliation, it is determined by one's existence as a part of human creation. Human creation is prone to battles. The first man and woman on

Earth had to battle temptation. And the battle was not their choice: the battle was their life. Life brings battles without option and suffering without reason as part of the human experience. So the question is not whether one is going to have battles, the question is whether one is going to succumb or confront their battles. To succumb is to give in, submit, surrender. To confront is to oppose, challenge, resist. Some people will not battle against temptation; they will surrender to their personal weaknesses. Yet, there are those who will contend with temptation. They will fight when they realize temptation is ruining their lives, disrupting their families, and causing serious unhappiness.

The reason I chose to concentrate on temptation is because I believe it is the root of all disruption in life. People's problems are urged and encouraged by temptation. The battle often centers on the fall rather than temptation. The fall is the thing whether substance, emotion, or spirit we've surrendered to (i.e. alcohol, drugs, sex, anger, or any other immoral, material or spiritual force in life). Temptation is the urging and feeling, pulling and thinking against one's will that leads to the fall. If we can control the urging and feeling that come with temptation, we can prevent the fall that results in unhappiness. When we prevent the fall, we don't suffer the consequences of our actions.

In other words, you're not battling alcohol or anger; you're battling against temptation because it is temptation that leads to alcohol and anger issues. If you can beat temptation, you can prevent the consequences of your fallen actions.

The book takes a direct tone, it is in the second person as in "You." The book uses God throughout for universal appeal; however, it is not without contextualizing Christ as the Son of God. Jesus says to the listeners in the book of Matthew chapter five while he is teaching from the mountainside: "when *you* pray", "when *you* fast", "when *you* give to the needy." Jesus was direct and without apology in his speech. He wanted to make it personal. He wanted each person to look at themselves and examine their weaknesses. This book wants to speak directly to "you." Put yourself in the text and read it with finger pointing at "you." Look at the weak you, the sinful you, the hostile you, the greedy you, or whatever "you" you may be suffering from as a result of your weakness. Although you cannot disinvite suffering into your life, you can cut down on suffering by confronting temptation which often results in suffering. If you're going to battle temptation, to end suffering and begin happiness, you need something to battle with.

# SOMETHING TO BATTLE WITH

*Life is, in fact, a battle. Evil is insolent and strong; beauty enchanting but rare; goodness very apt to be weak; folly very apt to be defiant; wickedness to carry the day; imbeciles to be in great places, people of sense in small, and mankind generally unhappy.*
*—Henry James*

## 1 Corinthians 3:9

Life is too short to live unhappy. Temptation and submission to weakness, crisis, and emotions can result in serious despondency. If you're going to be happy in life, you have to battle your weaknesses, confront your crises, and control your emotions all while building up your defenses against temptation. If you're going to battle temptation, you need something to battle with.

I want you to think of the scenario simply like this: You are in an actual battle for your life. The battle is between you and your opponent. You are fighting against your opposition and your opposition is fighting against you. The two of you are enemies. You are face to face with your enemy. Either you are going to fight your enemy or you are going to give in to your enemy. If you fight the enemy, you defend your life. If you give in to the enemy, you lose your life.

If you lose, the enemy takes control of your life. When the enemy takes control of your life, you are forced to do things you do not want to do. You will suffer until you regain control of your life. The only way to get back in control of your life is to battle against the enemy. If you are going to battle against the enemy, you need something to battle with.

Now think of this battle spiritually. You are forced to protect your mind, body, and soul. In this battle there is you and there is temptation. You are face to face with temptation. Either you are going to fight temptation or you are going to fall to temptation. If you fight temptation you stay in control of your life. If you fall to temptation you lose control of your life. When you lose control of your life the enemy takes control of your life.

When the enemy takes control of your life you are subjected to pain, punishment, and suffering. In order to regain control of your life you must battle temptation. In order to battle temptation you need something to battle with.

## Something to Battle Temptation

*Something to battle with* is simply equipment given to fight against temptation. For our purpose it is an actual and spiritual battle that impacts mind, body, soul, and feelings. *Something to battle with* means you need something to fight *with* and someone to go into battle *with* against your enemy. *No soldier goes to war without a weapon; they go into war with a weapon. No student goes to school without books; they should go to school with books.* The bible says "For we are labourers together *with* God" (1 Corinthians 3:9 KJV). God is our comrade, company, and companion in battle; therefore, when we go into battle we take God *with* us. When we take God with us, we have someone to battle against the enemy. God supplies all the tools needed in battle for our fight so that we have something to battle *with* when the enemy comes up against us.

This wording and phrasing may be semantically silly and even awkward to some people, because it challenges the typical understanding of us in battle. Many have come to believe they are battling with alcohol and battling with depression. However, I believe those who are battling are not battling *with* those forces but *against* them. To battle *with* gives a companion; to battle *against* gives an adversary. Why would anyone want to battle *with* the thing that's destroying them? You want to battle *against* the thing that's destroying you. Moses went into battle *with* God against Pharaoh. David went into battle *with* God against Goliath. David says in Psalm 23:4 "though I walk through the valley of the shadow of death, I will fear no evil: for thou art *with* me. . . ." Jesus says to the disciples when giving the great commission, "Surely I am *with* you always, to the very end of the age." (Matthew 28:20). The right wording gives proper distinction between one's friend in battle and one's enemy in battle.

Since we are in both a spiritual and actual battle we need both spiritual and practical tools to fight temptation. I don't want you to believe this book is so religious that it misses the reality of life. No! This book is practical so that it deals with the challenges of life. The challenges of life are real: from death and depression to sex and alcoholism. Real problems require real action and actual weapons to fight against temptation.

Temptation is a strong force that seeks to lure your body into wrongful submission. It is an urge, a feeling against your will, a grip against your control. Its purpose is to make you fall, transgress, commit an offense against your better judgment—a crime against divine will. It seeks to strip you of any consciousness or conviction of your wrongdoing. It can make you hurt without feelings, hate without caring and kill without conviction.

Temptation has a particular connotation—some may pin it to sin, and sin is an offense against God that must be acknowledged. We have all fallen short of the glory of God and temptation is the reason we have fallen. However, temptation also causes us to fall short in life. Falling short in life is submitting to influences that control our being. Those influences can be internal—such as fear, jealousy, and insecurity, as well as external—such as alcohol, food, and money. One can be tempted to give in to sickness, to accept weakness, and to partake in laziness. One can be tempted to holler, hit, kick, spit, and slap. Temptation induces a host of people, feelings, and actions. When we fall short in life, we also fall short of God's glory for our lives.

Temptation is crafty; it plays on your weakness. Temptation is tricky. It can fool you to make you believe it is good for you. It can look beautiful, feel wonderful, and even be helpful. It can love you, hug you, and kiss you, only to trap you and then bite you.

Temptation is a force from the enemy. The enemy is an adversary: satan, devil, demon, evil spirit, any opponent that operates against God's will for your life. David uses enemy as those actual persons who plot to hurt and harm him. In Psalms 140 – 143, David begs God to rescue him from his enemies: "Rescue me, O Lord, from evil men; protect me from men of violence" (Psalm 140:1 NIV). There is no doubt that enemy can be both spiritual and actual or spiritual wickedness operating through actual persons, possessions, emotions and substances. The enemy seeks to rob, steal, and destroy all that you are and all that God has for you. The enemy uses temptation to aid in your destruction. Once you fall to temptation, the force of temptation becomes harder to resist and easier to submit to. The more you submit, the weaker you get, the harder it is to quit. Once you fall, the consequences can be painful and even fatal to you and anyone connected to you. The enemy's ultimate goal for temptation is to make you suffer in your weakness and die with your demons.

## Faith, prayer, scripture, meditation, fasting

In order to prevent temptation's success, you need *something to battle with* that will build up your resistance against temptation. God is someone we go into battle *with* to fight against the enemy and God provides us *with* tools to fight against the enemy in battle: *Faith, Prayer, Scripture, Meditation,* and *Fasting* give you something to fight *with* in battle. They are not only spiritual possessions but actual weapons. Once we begin to see these spiritual possessions as actual and tangible tools to handle and hold, use and walk on, then we have something to go into battle with. We must convert *faith* into steps and walk on it as Abraham and Jesus did. We must change *prayer* into conversations and speak with it as Moses and Nehemiah did. We must transform *scripture* (the word of God) into weapons (sword of the spirit) and fight with it as Peter and Paul did. We must turn *meditation* into life and live with it as David did. We must transform *fasting* into ammunition and battle with it as Esther, Daniel, and Jesus did. When *faith*, *prayer*, *scripture*, *meditation*, and *fasting* become real in your life then you have *something to battle with*.

# You Need Faith in Battle
## (A Battle Ground)

*The God whom we worship is not a weak and incompetent God. He is able to beat back gigantic waves of opposition and to bring low prodigious mountains of evil. The ringing testimony of the Christian faith is that God is able.*
*—Rev. Dr. Martin Luther King, Jr.*

## Hebrews 11:1

You need faith to battle temptation. Faith is the ability to believe in someone other than yourself. God is other than yourself. What makes God other than yourself is that God is much bigger, better, and stronger than you. God is omnipotent, omniscient, and omnipresent. There is no one in existence like or even close to being like God. And if you're going to battle temptation you need someone much bigger, better, and stronger than you. Temptation is strong and you alone do not have the ability or strength to take on the enemy; if you did you wouldn't keep falling to temptation.

The enemy will fool you; will make you believe you can take on temptation, only to keep you from believing in God. When you don't believe in God, you believe only in you. Although it is good to believe in yourself and your abilities, it's a problem when you believe in *only* yourself and your abilities. The self alone is prone to weakness, sickness, and sadness, and therefore can be unreliable and limited in its ability to fight temptation. The enemy wants you to believe *only* in yourself because he knows you alone cannot beat temptation and he cannot beat God. The enemy will keep you from God to take advantage of your life. When the enemy takes control of your life he uses you for his own pleasure and then dumps you on the road of self-destruction. In order to avoid self-destruction you need to put your faith in someone other than yourself. When you put your faith in God you get the power needed to take on temptation. You get the knowledge needed to out-smart the enemy and you get a God that will never leave you or forsake you in battle.

When you put your faith in God, you put your trust in God, and when you put your trust in God, He takes off all the limitations that prevent you from winning the battle. In other words you are not going into battle alone, you are going into battle *with* a comrade who has proven to be the antithesis of evil, the nemesis of demons, and has a track record of rescuing people from self-destruction. When you have God on your side, the enemy is troubled and temptation is weakened. Your faith has given you strength and power beyond yourself.

## *Faith is actual, factual and practical*

Faith is the substance of things hoped for and the evidence of things not seen. In other words faith is for real. Faith has substance and evidence which makes it actual, factual, and practical. Faith is not only a conversational, theological, or orthodoxical concept but an *actual* construct. You can actually use faith in battle. Many people have taken faith to be only an invisible spiritual force and not an actual physical power. Faith is both spiritual force and actual element. Faith is substance and evidence that you can touch and feel, use and step on. It is your floor, your mat, your ground. In order for Jesus to walk on water he had to walk by faith (Matthew 14:25). Faith became the substance that kept him above the water. Therefore Jesus did not only walk on water; Jesus walked on faith over water. Jesus encouraged Peter to do the same and Peter began walking towards Jesus on the water but he got scared when he saw the storm and fell in the water. Peter didn't lose his step, he lost his faith. If Peter had kept his faith he would have overcome his fear and walked through the storm. What Jesus show us is that faith is for real. You can walk on faith. You can step on faith. Jesus never chastised Peter for falling in the water; Jesus questioned Peter's faith. If Peter had kept the faith, he would have made it through the storm and won the battle against fear.

Faith is *factual*; you can use faith for real, for good, to challenge doubt. Many people doubt God and doubt can prevent you from going into battle. Doubt is for real, people don't move when they have doubt or they move in the wrong direction. Doubt keeps you in your mess. Doubt hinders your faith. You must speak to God so that He helps you to overcome your disbelief.

Faith is *practical*: It will take you into battle even when you're doubtful. You can use faith to battle evil. Faith is what you use when you're going into battle. You don't go into battle empty-handed. Faith arms you for battle. It is a real weapon in battle against disbelief. And you're going to need to battle disbelief if you're going to fight the whole battle. Some people believe at first, like Peter, and then half way through the battle they lose faith. True faith keeps you fighting to the finish. With faith you can face life and face death. With faith you can fight for life and fight against death. Many people are afraid of death but faith conquers death like faith conquers life. Faith keeps you fighting to the very last breath.

Faith is a bed of mercy when you've fallen, a cup of tea when you're thirsty, and a sandwich when you're hungry. Faith is for real. It is a room when you're homeless. When you have faith you have the substance of your hope and the evidence of what's to come, and what's to come is victory over the enemy. You must believe that you have the victory because you hold faith.

Even when you fall you must believe you will win. Falling is not the end but rather part of the process towards the victory. All things work for the good, including the fall, when you're with God in battle. Everyone falls in life but not everyone gets up. Faith keeps you believing even when you've fallen. As a matter of fact the only way to get back up is by faith. Faith picks you up when you're down. Faith is your legs, your arms, your courage. Without faith you would stay down, cry in your pain, and wallow in your shame. But with faith you get up with your tears, fight the power in spite of your pain and run on regardless of your disgrace. Faith keeps you getting up every time you fall. Remember faith is for real. It provides the necessary substance needed for your restoration.

The worst thing you can do is fall and stay down. The reason why many people stay down is because they do not truly believe in God. God is a God of resurrection, not of despondence. When you put your faith in God, you turn everything over to God. Once you turn everything over to God, you receive power to rise above the enemy and face your battle with certainty. It's hard to battle cancer on your own. It's hard to battle a brain tumor, HIV/AIDS, or diabetes by yourself. You need something to take into battle. For this, God gives you faith and faith gives you strength to battle the unbeatable and win. And this win is not only physical but emotional, psychological, and spiritual.

With faith you can feel good no matter where you find yourself because God is with you. With faith you can hope no matter what happens in your life because God will never leave you. With faith you can believe in the impossible because God is present. When the enemy says *can't*, God makes a way. Where the enemy says *impossible*, God opens doors. All you have to do is believe that God can and God will.

Neither you nor anyone like you can battle alone against temptation and win. As you know people can be unpredictable and unreliable. They can be with you one minute and against you the next. They can be on your side in one battle and nowhere to be found the next round. The enemy can even use friends and family to tempt you rather than help you in battle. The enemy is shrewd, but God is faithful. When you put your faith in God there is a guarantee that God will always be with you; that God will never go up against you and God will never turn his back on you. God is with you in good times and in bad times, in sickness and in health, in poverty and in riches, in freedom and in prison.

God is faithful.

When you put your faith in God you never have to worry about God falling short—you have to worry about you falling short. Many of our problems and failures in life come from a lack of faith. We don't believe or trust God enough so we turn to other measures to save us, other people to rescue us, and other sources to deliver us. When you turn to someone or something other than God it shows your lack of faith and a lack of faith can lead to falling to temptation. The enemy loves those who lack faith because they will only go with God so far before they break away to do their own thing. And the enemy will travel with you until you've reached your limit with waiting on God, trusting in God, and believing in God. When you've reached your limit and your faith runs out, the enemy steps in where your faith left off and tempts you. The enemy will give you something other than God to believe in and use what has been given to cause havoc in your life. Instead of having one problem, you have more than one because you didn't have enough faith in God. You couldn't wait on God. You didn't go the distance with God.

When you feel like your faith is running out, you need to ask God to increase your faith. God can increase faith. God can increase your faith to help you go further in your battle. When you receive increased faith it gives you more patience to wait for the Lord, more truth to trust in God, and more courage to resist temptation. The truth is, at times you will be in your mess longer than you expect, and it will seem as if God is deaf and the enemy is all that's left. But faith is able to extend beyond the length of your suffering. Faith knows how to wait on God. When you are able to go the distance with God, it not only shows that God is with you but that you are with God. And in order to be with God you must have faith.

When you take faith into battle it gives you peace in the midst of war and relief in the midst of combat because you realize that God is fighting your battle. This battle is not yours but God's. When God fights the battle you can feel like a winner because you know God has never lost a battle. Faith gives you a winning spirit. It makes you feel like you can beat anything in you or coming at you. After each battle your faith should be increased and your confidence boosted—all because you've overcome temptation and regained your life.

For instance, if you've battled alcohol and beaten alcohol, your faith should be increased and your confidence boosted. You should feel good about yourself because if it had not been for your faith in God, you would have never beaten alcohol.

## Many people…

The feeling of confidence and reassurance as a result of faith will lead you to challenge things and do the things you once feared. The enemy uses fear to inhibit our progress and prevent our success. *Many people* have missed out on dreams and goals because of fear. Many people are too afraid to step outside their homes, step outside their community, step outside their culture—all because of fear. Fear is a great source of regret and frustration in many people's lives. And it is a shame when someone misses out on life and all the blessings that God has for them because they cower in fear.

However, when you have God on your side you walk by faith and not by fear. Remember: Faith is for real. It is a step when you see no step. It is a ground when you see no ground. Faith challenges fear by taking you beyond your limitations into possibilities that God has planned for your life. When you have faith in God you trust that wherever you go God will be with you; God's wings will protect you and God's angels will watch over you. When you have faith in God you step outside your limitations and go beyond your boundaries and believe that God has something good waiting for you.

*Many people* will not step out on faith but will be kicked out by force. Don't get mad, this may be God's plan for your life. God may need to kick you out of your current job, marriage or home so that you can learn to walk by faith. Some people will never become the person that they ought to be until they get kicked out of their comfort zone.

You will never get out of where you are and get to where God wants you to be if you don't get pushed out. However, the brutal is not always that bad. All things work for the good of those that love the Lord. The good thing about God is that even when you get kicked out, you still land on faith. When Peter fell in the water Jesus caught him. God will catch you whether you step out or get kicked out and it's up to you to learn to walk by faith whichever way you come out.

*Many people* restrict themselves because of limited resources. They allow their lack of finances to determine their length of progress. However, when you have faith in God your income does not decide your outcome. God can take the little or the nothing that you have and put you through college. With faith God can consolidate every bill and take you from broke and bankrupt to being financially stable and debt free. With faith you can buy a house or a car with no money down. God is able. When you step out on faith God will send you to the right people and places to make the impossible, possible. The shortage of cash does not stop you from going the distance with God. The only thing that stops you is your lack of faith. You have to believe and get beyond your limits and enter into God's abundance. Money doesn't control God, God controls money. God can get you to where you need to be with or without money. The Lord will be your refuge and strength, your food and shelter. Faith in God can take you to places you've never been and introduce you to people you've never met.

*Many people* are afraid because they don't want to go alone. Some people always need someone to go with them. But faith is your friend. You don't need anybody else if you have faith in God. Faith is a real friend. God may want you to go alone to show you things that are just for you and if you take someone else you may focus on them and miss what God is showing you. People can block your blessing.

Faith is your most necessary weapon against the enemy because you can't go into battle without it. Faith is the core of all things possible in God, and so without faith nothing is possible.

In order to please God you must have faith because without faith it is impossible to please God. To please God is to show that you have indeed used your faith to give God glory and resist temptation. To please God is to make God proud because you fight hard and strong against the enemy; you fall but get back up, you get scared but keep fighting, you are wounded but keep the faith. And there is no doubt you will get wounded and scarred in battle against the enemy. Cancer can wound and scar you mentally, physically and spiritually. Your scars will be seen on your body, by the loss of your hair and by the dysfunction of some of your faculties. However, it's better to come through the battle wounded than to not come through the battle at all. Your wounds show that you put up a good fight and that the enemy couldn't take you down easily. You didn't give into sorrow. You didn't allow pain and weakness to have the final word. You didn't allow physical changes to your body to steal your fight for life and living. You fought the good fight. You kept the faith.

God allows wounds and scars in battle so that we can remember all that we've been through but also all that we've made it through. The latter allows us to be grateful and more faithful to God for bringing us through the battle, wounds and all. When you make it through, your wounds are no longer a sign of sickness but a sign of victory. You have the victory! The victory should make you feel good, beautiful and worthy. You made it! You kept the faith! When you keep the faith it means you never let go of God's hand, you keep holding on, you keep trusting and believing in God. Our lives should be spent pleasing God since God's life is spent fighting our battles. If someone is doing something for you, the least you can do is make them proud. God is doing so much for us in battle the least we can do is fight with all our faith.

The good thing about faith is that all you need is a mustard seed and with this mustard seed you can move mountains. When you can move mountains you can challenge the biggest problem in your life and believe that God will deliver. You can challenge the strongest temptation and believe that God will strengthen. You can face the toughest dilemma and believe that God will answer. You can be in the worse condition and sing because you have not allowed horrific conditions to steal your happiness. Many people surrender their joy to surrounding circumstances as if God cannot handle bad conditions. However, the faithful keep on singing in the midst of the worse because they know that God is able to beat any and all challenges. With faith you can challenge sickness and weakness but also the absence of happiness. Faith keeps you smiling and laughing in the midst of suffering.

You can actually walk through suffering with faith. Whether you're suffering because of loss or because of consequences it can be exhausting spiritually, physically and emotionally. It can rob you of all the strength you have in the bank of divinity. Many people have actually begun to believe in their suffering over their faith in God. To believe in suffering is to submit to its powers and surrender to its sorrows. However, while suffering is draining faith is enabling. Faith keeps you believing there is a way out of suffering to a greater hope and happiness. While suffering is paralyzing faith is energizing. Faith actually picks you up and pushes you on, up and out of darkness. Faith keeps the lamp on. Faith actually gives you light to see better, comfort to feel better and hope to think better. The best counter punch to suffering is faith.

## *Prayer, scripture, meditation and fasting require faith*

Finally, everything you do in life must be backed by faith. Faith must be real.

You can't *pray* without faith. Prayer without faith is a hollow tune signifying nothing. In other words God won't hear a prayer that is not backed by faith. How can you speak to God and not believe in Him? How can you hear from God if you don't have faith in Him? You have to believe that God is able and obtainable if you're going to talk to Him. You have to believe that there is nothing too hard for God if you're going to call on Him in battle. Faith makes prayer real.

You can't read the *word of God* without faith. A lot of people don't believe the word of God because they have no faith. In order to really capture the essence and existence of God, it takes faith. How can you read about and be affected by the creation, the opening of the Red Sea, the walking on water, the resurrection, and the return of God without faith? You need faith to engage in the scriptures or else you're just reading a story. When you're just reading a story it's more entertaining than edifying. Faith makes scripture real.

You need faith to *meditate* on God's goodness.

God's goodness is all that God is and all that God gives. God's goodness is filled with power, mercy, grace, love, forgiveness, peace and joy. You need faith to believe in all of God and receive all of God. When you meditate, God's goodness flows from Him to you and when God's goodness flows to us we walk by faith and not by sight. Faith makes meditation real.

You must have faith to *fast*. Fasting is the ability to give up something you crave and deny the flesh its desires. When you give up something for God you must believe that God will provide and supply all your needs. Fasting gives you the ability to worship God in spirit and truth. If we are to speak to God, we must speak in the spirit. If we are to believe in God we must believe He is the truth. The truth is there is nothing too hard for God. The truth is the enemy cannot beat God and temptation has no influence when God is on your side. The truth is every knee shall bow to God. You have to believe in God's very existence and attributes in order to serve Him. You can't serve God without faith. When faith is real everything connected to faith becomes real. Faith makes *prayer, scripture, meditation* and *fasting* real in your life. They are not unseen or obscure means to an end they are actual possessions (like a gun or knife) in battle.

Faith is the substance of things hoped for and the evidence of things not seen.

# You Need Prayer in Battle
## (A Bullhorn)

*May the Lord save you from any painful regrets when the reaping time shall come. But may you all have so lived, that no arrow from God's quiver of justice can pierce your soul, nor mountain of guilt sink you down. But may you all find your portion, with the redeemed and sanctified out of every nation, tongue and people, around the burnished throne of God, with everlasting shouts of joy and praise upon your lips. Amen*
*—Anthony Binga, Jr.*

## Luke 22:40

You need prayer to battle temptation. Prayer is communing with someone other than yourself. The reason why you need to commune with someone other than yourself is because temptation talks to you. Temptation tells you what to do. Temptation is a feeling against your will and a thought against your thinking. It tells you to do things you should not do and blocks any communication that may free you. Many people submit to temptation because that's the only voice they hear. And when that's the only voice you hear, that's the only voice you follow.

Prayer gives an alternative voice to temptation. Prayer gives you an opportunity to go outside of yourself and speak to God. When you speak to God, you set up a face-to-face battle between God and temptation. In fact, the best time to pray is when you are face to face with temptation. As soon as you feel temptation coming on, pray.

Prayer speaks in the opposite direction of your temptation. Prayer talks out against temptation. When temptation urges you to commit the offense, your prayer speaks to God about resisting the offense. When temptation says *Go*, your prayer should say *No! Don't go!* When temptation says *Do it*, your prayer should say *No! Don't do it!* Prayer is for real. It is your phone, your bullhorn, your line of communication to God. When you pray you actually talk to God and talk against the enemy. When you pray God actually listens and talks to you. You must learn to pray for what's right and speak against what's wrong. You must learn to pray to God so you can recognize your weakness. Many live in denial and the darkness of their weakness— unwilling to admit there is a problem with temptation. Prayer helps you identify your flaws and confess your wrongs so that you become a better person.

Many people find it hard to pray. But if you can speak from your heart and think from your head you can pray. You can pray soft as a whisper or loud as a shout—whatever you feel is your need in that moment. There are some prayers that require silence, and there are certain prayers that require noise. The good thing about prayer is that it is effective anyway you say it as long as it is coming from God. Yes, prayer comes from God. God will put the right words in your mouth at the right time to deal with what's wrong. Don't try and tell God what you want, ask God for what you need.

Some people wake up with a silent prayer, a prayer strictly between them and God. They just want to talk to God about what's going in their lives; they want to beg forgiveness and voice their gratefulness.

Yet others go throughout the day and night with a more thunderous prayer, loud and clear, like a bullhorn, so the enemy can hear. Their prayer is also talking directly to the enemy, *Away from me, Satan!* And this is indeed a battle prayer. When you begin to pray against the enemy, you call God into the battle. You are calling for strength to resist temptation. You may want to get out of the battle, but God may need you to fight the battle. God will give you the words to speak to

Him and the answer when He speaks to you.

As previously stated, the best time to pray is when temptation is present. When temptation is present, it makes your conversation with God easier because you see exactly what you're praying against. If you know what your weakness is, praying is simply talking against the temptation and seeking God for strength and resistance. When something is tempting you, you pray: *Help me, Lord, to resist this cake. Help me, Lord, to resist this woman. Help me, Lord, to resist this man. Help me, Lord, to be patient.*

## Prayer of resistance, forgiveness, persistence, happiness and faithfulness

Prayer calls attention to your weakness and cries to God for *resistance.* The more you recognize your weakness, the more you pray against it, the more you can resist it. Resisting temptation is the greatest conversation you can have with God because it relieves you of any pain and suffering that come with transgression. If you can resist temptation, you don't have to worry about the consequences of your actions. No fall, no bad consequence. It is great when you can walk away, run away, or shout down your temptation because it gives you control over your actions and when you have control over your actions you live happier.

However, you will fall to temptation. Everyone is battling against something and will most likely find themselves failing at one time or another. And when you fall you will suffer the consequences of your actions. However, suffering can also revive us with the greatest prayer. The more you suffer, the greater the prayer. It is often after the fall we feel the most pain, shame, anger, and persistent worry.

What greater time to pray than after the offense? Your prayer should be a prayer of *forgiveness.* You need to talk to God about forgiveness. Forgiveness says that you didn't like what you did and would like to never do it again. Forgiveness lets God know you recognize you're wrong and would like to be pardoned for your transgression.

When you pray not only does God hear you but the enemy hears you as well. The enemy realizes that although you fell, you are conscious of your fall and are putting temptation on notice: *You are willing to battle to prevent falling again.* Pray for strength when you fall so that you do not fall again. Pray for self-control so that you stay in control of your life. Pray that the consequences of your fall are not that great and the suffering is not that long. Prayer after the fall is the most faithful prayer because it is fighting against fear.

The enemy would love for you to walk around in fear as a result of your fall because fear troubles faith. But faithful prayer speaks to fear and hands over your worry to God. Prayer without faith is worthless and will only result in greater suffering. Faith gives prayer backing and will result in greater overcoming. Prayer helps you to remember the suffering that came as a result of your fall so that you don't fall again and have to suffer again.

However, the truth is most people will fall over and over again. They suffer the consequences but the temptation is so strong that they recommit the crime. This is a real problem with weakness and can disturb happiness and be fatal. The worst offenders are those who are conscious of their offenses but continue to fall to temptation. But a great struggle is going on in the transgressor; a war between right and wrong, good and evil.

Constant falls are also the best time for *persistent* prayers. And *persistent* praying sets up a real battle between God and temptation. The awareness and regret of the offender make the battle real and make the praying relentless. The constant praying keeps God in the battle. The recidivist can possibly be the most ardent prayer-warrior if after and before every wrongdoing he prays. If there is a prayer of resistance before the offense and a prayer of forgiveness after the offense this makes for a great prayer-warrior. If the offender remains persistent and never gives up regardless of how many times a crime is committed, faithfulness will pay off. You must keep praying regardless of your weakness. With faithfulness God will show Himself mighty and strong.

However, many will suffer permanent punishment because of their transgression. The result of falling to temptation can be enduring disease, injury, and loss. After the offense leaves them in a permanent state of brokenness, some people give up because they feel they have lost everything or that there is nothing to live for. Others lose hope, faith, and trust in God, themselves, and everyone around them. The enemy wins when you lose and stay down. The enemy loves it when you lose faith in God and everyone around you as a result of your perpetual feeling.

But the strongest prayer is when you can talk to God about light in the midst of darkness, hope in the midst of despair, and strength in the midst of brokenness. Yes, you may be in a permanent state of loss as a result of your fall, but that does not mean your situation should destroy your life. You can still live. As long as you have breath, you can talk to God. Talk to God about how to live in your new state. The greatest battle comes when you can talk to God about finding *happiness* in the midst of sadness. Many people are living happy lives with disease, after divorce or life imprisonment. They've learned to live with God rather than live with fault, and when you live with God you see things differently.

You don't need to look at life through the lens of your suffering, you can look at it from the perspective of God's promise to always be present, no matter what happens. While the enemy puts your mind on the worse of your condition, God turns your eyes to the work of his perfection. God can still use you and renew you for his wonder. I've seen people learn to run with one leg, see with one eye, and live longer than expected with chronic diseases. There are people who find purpose in prison, happiness in the hospital, and pleasure after impotence. God is not limited in what He can do with whatever condition you find yourself in. There is nothing too hard for God.

Most of all, God can work the emotions. Emotions are why most people suffer. Many people fall into deep despair and depression; many don't care if they live or die. This is an emotionally-doomed and dark state. If you don't care if you live or die you have lost all meaning in life; you have discarded what is sacred. When you discard what is sacred you discard God, who gave you life. Your life is to be cherished and used for God's purpose, whatever state you find yourself in. But the enemy can make you believe your life is worthless. When you believe your life is worthless you have no problem committing suicide, or drinking yourself to death, or doing something careless to wreck your life. The enemy loves it when people go down this road because it shows they have neither the light of God to guide them nor the presence of God to keep them.

This is the enemy's best time to tempt, but it's also God's best time to work.

Believe it or not this is where God operates best, if you just look to God for a moment. If you find the energy to mumble out a little prayer of faith, you will see God is able to restore you to your senses. You will see that God is with you in your crisis. God will show you His glory and mercy. God's grace will step in and pull you out of foolish thinking and return you to wisdom. God's mercy will bring you from worthlessness to worthiness. God's love will rescue you from sin and suicidal thinking and place you on a rock of revival. All it takes is one *faithful* prayer, which God will give you to save yourself.

God loves us so much that if we don't have the prayer or the strength to look to Him, He gives us the very prayer to talk to Him. He gives us the strength to look to Him. He gives us the faith to believe in Him. What a mighty God we serve!

This is God's grace: when we don't have it, He brings it. When we can't make it, He steps in. With a faithful prayer God can turn sadness to laughter and pain to joy. Pray to God for a bright side. There is a bright side somewhere as long as you have breath in your body. The permanent condition may be a result of your transgression but also a reminder of God's power. It can help you and you can help others. When others see you they can be cautious and encouraged—cautious not to fall to temptation and encouraged that God still works when you're at your worst.

Prayer takes practice and discipline. The best time to pray is when you get up in the morning. Why? Because God woke you up. God didn't have to wake you up. Wake up a little earlier to pray. Just as you would talk on the phone for hours, talk to God. Prayer has nothing to do with the amount of time or times you pray, it has to do with the quality of your faith. You don't want to get up from your prayer until you feel that God has spoken, particularly if you are dealing with a stressful situation. The more faith you have in God when you pray and after you pray the less time you will be on your knees. However, the less faith you have in God when you pray the longer you will feel stress and discomfort because without faith your issues remain with you. Your weakness will stay with you until you can pray and truly turn your situation over to God. Only then can you get up and faithfully walk away.

Don't give God time only because you have nothing else to do, God deserves the time He has given you. Make time for God. Don't get interrupted by others or phone calls, give God His time since God gave you time when He woke you up. You have a reason to pray no matter how tired or busy you are. Pray to fight weariness and busyness. Pray before you talk on the phone, get on the computer, watch the television, or read the daily paper.

If you really want to discipline yourself, talk to God before you talk to anyone else. *Good morning, God.* People are going to get upset when you start giving God time because its time you used to give to them. But pray for them, they'll get used to it if you don't give up; if they don't, God has answered your prayer.

Prayer should be disciplined and daily. Pray sitting up or kneeling down. Try not to pray in the bed while you're laying down; you will only give in to sleep's temptation. The enemy would love for you to fall asleep during prayer. When you fall asleep, you can miss the answer to your prayer. Discipline yourself. Kneel by the bed or in the bathroom since that's the first place most people go after they wake up. When you pray, humble yourself. Don't take God for granted. The way to talk to God is with humility and meekness. Don't get arrogant and demanding.

Remember, you don't know what can happen in a day. You don't know what temptation has planned for you. Before you woke up, the enemy was already up planning your fall. You want to pray before you step out the door. You want to walk out ready for battle. Prayer gets you ready for battle. Pray for patience. Pray for silence. Pray for understanding. Pray for wisdom. Prayerful preparation helps you prior to temptation. The patience will help you with anger. The silence will help you with conversation. The understanding will help you with imbeciles and the wisdom will help you with decisions. Pray for your health and God's protection. Pray for your family that God protects them from all hurt, harm, and danger. Pray for your enemies that God shows you how or how not to deal with them. Pray for advanced resistance and forgiveness against temptation.

Practice prayer as you go throughout the day. Don't always wait to pray when something happens, pray to prevent something from happening. Pray just to pray so that you make up for all the times you didn't pray. If you pray always, then it will become part of your daily regimen, so even if you forget to pray in the morning, you will find yourself pausing to pray some time throughout the day. You want to make prayer a permanent part of you. As you go throughout the day, you have ample opportunities to practice praying. Something in that day is going to make you pray. Pray before you eat, while you're working, when you run to the bathroom. Pray before the meeting, after the meeting, in the midst of the meeting.

The good thing about prayer is that it can interrupt any conversation. If you say something you should not have said, pray for forgiveness. Prayer can interrupt any thought. If you thought something you should not be thinking, pray over it. Situations will arise throughout the day that make you worry, scared, and angry. The enemy would love for you to drown in your emotions but the situation should drive you toward devotion. While you're worried, scared, and angry don't go further into your negative emotions, distance yourself from them by praying. This is a good time to pray for relief. Don't stop praying until you feel relieved of your worry, fear, or anger.

Sufficient prayer has a way of tackling the root of the problem that triggered your emotions so that you can defeat the enemy and feel God's presence over whatever caused your worry. Don't rush through prayer, or else you'll get up feeling the same way as when you went down. Give time to feel God and hear God and empty your head and heart of what's bothering you. Make time for prayer. The more you practice, the more you will be prepared to deal with temptation when it comes your way.

Finally, don't forget to be thankful in prayer. You can pray a prayer of thanksgiving before you go to sleep. Thank God for getting you through another the day. No matter how tough it was, you still made it by the grace of God. You may have fallen, you may have slipped, but God still brought you through. Before you go to sleep, there should be a prayer of reflection, forgiveness, and thanksgiving. In all things give thanks; that is give thanks for the good and the bad, the rise and the fall because God brought you through it all.

Don't underestimate prayer as a potent force to be used in any and every situation. While you're praying, you're talking to God, and you're releasing your stress and anger and any discomfort you may have with life. Some people go crazy because they have no one to talk to. Many people find themselves breaking down and crying to themselves every night. Life can be so exasperating and exhausting, so unfair and cruel, but God is *so* good. God opens his ear to every care we have and every word we speak.

Everybody needs somebody to talk to; thank God we can *take it to the Lord in prayer*. We can take our frustrations, annoyances and dilemmas to God. God allows us to share every temperament with Him. Every attitude He accepts. When you talk to God and confess your sins you don't have to worry about God spreading your business to anyone. God is a safe keeper; you can trust God with all your information. Prayer is found throughout the Bible by every prophet, priest, and king, by every servant of God. Read your Bible and study the scriptures and you will see.

# YOU NEED SCRIPTURE IN BATTLE
# (A SWORD)

*How useful soever this book of book is in itself, It will
be of no use if we do not acquaint ourselves with it, by
reading it daily, and meditating upon it, that we may
understand the mind of God in it, and may apply what
we understand to ourselves for our direction, rebuke, and
comfort, as there is occasion. It is the character of the holy
and happy man that his delight is in the law of the Lord;
and, as an evidence thereof, he converses with it as his
constant companion, and advises with it as his most wise
and trusty counsellor, for in that law doth he meditate
day and night, Ps.1:2*
*— Matthew Henry*

## 2 Timothy 3:16

You need scripture to battle temptation. Scripture is the written
word of God. It contains information, inspiration, and instructions
beyond what you already have to support your fight. If you are going
to battle temptation you need words that will inform you, inspire you,
and instruct you in life. The enemy's words are full of misinformation, disempowerment, and misdirection, which all will only lead to
your destruction. If you're going to battle the enemy you need words
beyond the enemy's words. You need the word of God. When you get
the word of God it battles the enemy's words and builds up resistance
to temptation.

Once you've learned the scriptures, they will enter your mind and replace filth that clogs your head. Lustful thoughts are challenged by the word of God. Evil thoughts are challenged by the word of God. Arrogant thinking is challenged by the word of God. The more you read the better you battle. The word of God goes from your head to your heart. Your heart is a living organism that pumps blood throughout your body and keeps you living. The scripture is a living word that pumps God throughout your body and keeps you fighting. When you live for the Lord, you no longer live for the enemy. The enemy must be evicted from your life so that you may properly dispense the good of God from your heart. In order to properly dispense the good of God, you must cut the enemy out of your life. The word of God is for real; it can actually cut the enemy out of your life. This is a real battle, when you cut the enemy out. The word of God is referred to as the sword of the spirit because it cuts temptation as soon as it arises. The word cuts at the enemy, who is the root of evil.

The best time to use the scripture is when temptation is present. While temptation seeks your fall, scripture seeks your resurrection by countering the enemy's claims on your life. When the enemy says one thing, the word of God says another. When the enemy does one thing the word of God does another.

The scriptures are filled with stories of hope and overcoming that can be used for your inspiration. The word of God contains characters that God has used to fight his battles and that you can use to fight yours. The word of God is filled with poetic principles that you can recite for your daily devotion. Each story, character, and poem is used to sharpen your blade and cut down temptation. And the goal for any man or woman of God is to cut down temptation. You don't want to be filled with things that can easily tempt you and ruin you.

Some people are so easily tempted by anything. They will eat anything, sleep with anything, drink anything, get angry over anything, can't wait for anything, and don't listen to anything. When you are so easily tempted by anything, it is a serious problem that the enemy enjoys but God abhors. God does not like to see his people suffer so

God contends with the enemy through his word. God gives people the sword, which is the word of God, so that they can cut down anything coming at them. This is a real battle.

When you are able to cut down anything you are also able to cut down suffering in your life. When you cut down suffering you cut down the chains that bind you and free yourself from temptation's control. When you free yourself from temptation's control you are no longer identified with your past mistakes rather you are aligned with your present success. Many people have made the mistake of identifying themselves with their former lives as addicts, alcoholics, and ex-convicts.

This is not the word of God.

According to the scripture, if you have been set free, you are free indeed. "So if the Son sets you free, you will be free indeed" (John 8:36 NIV). When you are free indeed you don't identify yourself with your failure, you identify yourself with your freedom. *Free indeed* erases your past so you can live in your present and move towards a greater future. Your latter life in God will be better than your former life in sin. You are a conqueror, an overcomer, a survivor, a valiant soldier. Words are significant, and how you describe yourself is important to your future aspirations and connections. You are connected to God and God is power. The word of God gives you information which tells you that you are more than a conqueror. "In all these things we are more than conquerors through him that loved us" (Romans 8:37 KJV). When you are a conqueror you have crushed your addiction into oblivion and are no longer associated with its remnants. When you are a conqueror you feel confident and secure in yourself as a person. God's word has a way of boosting your self-esteem and worth. God's word makes you feel like somebody, and the better you feel the better you fight.

Not only do you cut down temptation coming at you, but you also cut down temptation within yourself. As stated, the sword cuts at the root of the problem. The root of the problem is evil. Evil seeks to make you break your promise to God, but the scripture reminds you of your commitment to God and yourself. When you read the scriptures you are also soaking in the word of God. Every word is a promise. Every verse is a commitment to live God's word.

Many people make promises (*I will never drink again. I will never smoke again. I will never lie again.*) only to break them later. However, when you make a promise to God, you must keep it. Your word is your bond. When you live God's word you live against temptation and fight against evil. When you break that commitment you feel the break in your promise and the crime against divinity. The feeling is one of guilt and humiliation and can sentence you to hopelessness, anguish, and isolation. A broken promise can haunt you to remind you of your pledge to God and to yourself. The feeling should lead you back to God's word to beg forgiveness, to seek righteousness, and to recommit yourself to His promise.

The enemy would love for you to be chewed by guilt and swallowed by disgrace. It will only make your sentence with the absurd much longer. The enemy can make you feel so bad that you feel like you can't get up the strength to come back to God. But the word of God is for those who have fallen. The scripture is for those who feel guilt and shame. If you break your promise: *Get up, go to God, beg forgiveness and renew your pledge.*

You have to find a verse that supports your forgiveness and brings you back to God's goodness. This is how you can determine whether or not temptation has been cut down in your life—when you are able to get up the strength to come back to God regardless of how awful you feel and how hard you fell. When you do get up, it shows the word of God pumping throughout your body is real.

Many people have a hard time reading, particularly reading the word of God. The enemy would love for you to use this as an excuse because he knows the word of God is power against temptation. And if you lack this weapon, you can easily lose the whole battle. Many people wonder why they can't fight their addiction, can't combat their depression or anger; it's because they have not taken the scripture with them in battle. As stated, if you are going to battle you need something to battle with, you can't go into battle empty-headed. Scripture fills your mind with words that give you strength over your addiction, hope over your depression, and power over your temper. The word of God is for real.

But if you use excuses not to read the scriptures you've already lost the battle. And if you've lost the battle you no longer have control of your life. Excuses are tricks from the enemy to make you feel defeated. Once you feel defeated you have no way out of your condition and will most likely remain there and God forbid die there. The enemy fears you may hear the word of God and gain power to fight temptation. You may read the word of God and gain access to information that gives you victory over the enemy. So the enemy will keep you believing that your reading is not strong enough to understand the verses, that your mind is too weak to remember the stories or to recite the poetry, that there is nothing in the scriptures that can help you. The devil is a liar and will use any attack to keep you defeated. If you read the word of God you will see that the enemy is shrewd but God is smarter; the enemy is powerful but God is stronger and the enemy can't do anything without God's permission. God protects his people from their enemies.

If you read the word of God, temptation is resisted and the enemy is rejected all because of the power of God. No wonder the enemy would want to keep the scriptures from you because the word of God tells of the enemy's weakness, temptation's resistance, and God's protection. You need the word of God if you're going to fight this battle.

There are many ways to gain understanding of scripture. You can listen for scripture. Go into a house of worship and listen to sermons and the scripture that is being read for that day. Once you hear it, write it down and go home and re-read it. Sometimes all it takes is one message to get you going. With today's technology there are ample ways to gain access to the word of God. There are CDs, DVDs, apps and other tech devices that can help you.

There are many versions to the bible that make reading it simple and understandable. If you find the King James Version too difficult to grasp, read the New International Version or the New King James Version, or the New Living Translation Bible, or the New American Standard Bible, or the English Revised Version. There are bibles that cater to Men and Women and Youth and Children. There are bibles with commentaries and definitions and geography, etc. There is no excuse not to engage in the Word of God.

But don't just listen to it or look at it, you want to absorb it. You want to get it in your spirit. Many people read but they don't understand the word of God. You want to read until you get a firm understanding of the scripture. Don't get up until the story you're reading, the verse you're looking at, the psalm you're reciting is deep in your soul and steep in your mind. The bible is broken down into stories of people and events that you can read over and over again until you get a clear understanding of it. Only when you truly understand it will you be able to speak it and live it.

The purpose of the word of God is to know it so you can use it. The scripture says "Study to shew thyself approved unto God, a workman that needeth not to be ashamed, rightly dividing the word of truth" (2 Timothy 2:15 KJV). The word of God is the word of truth and you must study to prove what you know. You must study any reading that can nourish your soul and strengthen your mind against temptation. Study is reading towards understanding. Don't set your reading aside until you totally understand that which you have read. Study the scriptures but also study any reading that will enhance your knowledge and broaden your intellect. Read the newspaper, read religious and not religious books, read history, politics and culture. The only way you prove what you know is to study. Read it so you can live it.

You have to read scripture over and over again until what's read is a part of your life and dripping from your mouth. You want to be able to interrupt a conversation and refer to the word of God. You want to be able to speak and recite the word of God. You want to be in a crowd and debate the word of God. When the word is in you, you can't help but speak it. The scripture puts the right words in your mouth so you don't have to say the wrong thing. Many people suffer with a bad mouth. They cuss loud and talk tough. They don't think before they speak. As a result they find themselves constantly in trouble because of what was said. When you swallow the word of God, you think before you speak and talk with respect and dignity. The word of God keeps the words you speak wholesome and holy.

The enemy can show up at any time, so the more you know, the better you battle. Many people are ill-equipped to deal with the enemy; they have one verse that they use for every situation. And that one verse may be able to get you through some temptations but not necessarily all. The enemy is tricky and comes at you in different ways. If he knows he can't succeed in one way he'll come at you another. The enemy can act differently, look different, talk differently, and even walk differently just to get your attention. You have to be ready no matter which way the enemy comes. And the best way to be ready is to study and have enough scriptures to go into battle with.

If you've ever been in a battle for your life you will know that extra ammunition is a must. Doctors know that some medicines are ineffective against certain diseases, so they prescribe a more potent medicine to deal with the sickness. They have a backup plan just in case one prescription does not work. With the multitude of scriptures, you have more than enough ammunition to fight your battles. Just in case the enemy decides to come from the back rather than the front, the left over the right. The more you study, the more scriptures you can use to push back the enemy and cut down temptation. One bucket of water can't put out a big fire; you need a hose that has endless water flowing out. The word of God has endless scriptures flowing out.

The word of God prepares you for the reality of life. Many people are fooled into believing because they serve God they will have no problems. This is not the reality. How do you prove God is real if you have no problems? If you read the scriptures you will see that God's servants had enemies. God's servants had disappointments. God's servants failed and sinned and cried and bled. When you study the word of God you will realize that walking with Him is not easy. It can be difficult and tumultuous, slippery and dangerous. When some people find out they face the same troubles with God as without God, maybe even more difficulties with God than without God, they decide to leave God. But God's word never said you would have no troubles, God's word says He will never leave you alone in trouble. "I will never leave you nor forsake you" (Joshua 1:5 NIV).

With God you have someone to battle with; without God you go it alone. And when you battle alone you lose because you don't have the strength alone to battle the enemy. You will have enemies but according to the word of God, God can turn your enemies into your footstool. You will fall down but God can use your fall for your resurrection. You will have disappointments, but the scripture says "weeping may endure for a night but joy cometh in the morning" (Psalm 30:5 KJV). Disappointments often come from our expectations exceeding or ignoring God's promise. God's promise is that He will never leave us in battle, however many have mistaken God's word to suggest He will never lead us into battle. We get disappointed when we find ourselves in battles and things don't work out the way we hoped they would. We presume that God should give us what we want and when we don't get it we get upset at God. What we fail to realize is that God doesn't owe us anything; we owe God. And because we owe God we must believe whatever we receive or don't receive is part of God's plan for our lives.

God is looking out for you. God knows best. God sees ahead. God can prevent us from getting some things because they may be dangerous and disastrous for our natural and spiritual lives. You may want that car or job but God may say no in order to protect you from a greater danger that comes with your desire. We often fail to understand that the things we want but don't get can be God protecting us from something worse. God's promise is not contingent upon what we receive or don't receive. God's promise is based upon His protection and presence, His power and authority over evil. And the enemy will tempt you into accepting that which God has rejected for your life. When you fall to temptation, you set yourself up for greater problems. There are people who will accept anything out of loneliness, desperation and boredom. And the enemy can make what you want look and sound so good that it's hard to resist. You have to be real careful not to accept everything that looks good. The word of God tells us that "whatever is true, whatever is noble, whatever is right, whatever is pure, whatever is lovely, whatever is admirable – if anything is excellent or praiseworthy – think about such things" (Philippians 4:8 NIV). We have to think about such things to make sure what we get is from God and not from the enemy.

## When feeling?_____ read...

That's why daily reading is essential; it equips you for whatever may come that day. The best way to know if you understand the word of God is to use it. You have to use what you've learned. When temptation comes, use the word of God. Counter the enemy's claims against your life with the sword. Get a verse that resonates with your problem; that gives you power against temptation. *When feeling* weak and worthless you can read "I can do all things through Christ which strengthens me" (Philippians 4:13 KJV). *When feeling* frustrated and disappointed you can read "weeping may endure for a night but joy cometh in the morning" (Psalm 30:5 KJV). *When feeling* scared and alone you can recite "The Lord is my light and my salvation; of whom shall I fear? The Lord is the strength of my life; of whom shall I be afraid?" (Psalm 27: 1 KJV). *When feeling* uncertain about the presence and the power of God you can read "I know that my Redeemer lives, and that in the end he will stand upon the earth" (Job 19: 25 NIV). *When feeling* thankful and praiseful recite "Let everything that has breath praise the Lord. Praise the Lord" (Psalm 150 NIV).

*When feeling* prayerful recite Matthew 6: 9-13 "Our father who art in heaven, hallowed be thy name, thy kingdom come thy will be done on earth as it is in heaven..." *When feeling* guilty and sinful because of others read, "Do not be misled "Bad Company corrupts good character." Come back to your senses as you ought, and stop sinning; for there are some who are ignorant of God – I say this to shame you" (1 Corinthians 15: 33-34 NIV). When you feel sick and helpless read the story of the sick woman and the man with the sick daughter (Matthew 9:18-26). *When feeling* tempted to do wrong you can shout "Away from me, Satan!" (Matthew 4:10 NIV). When the enemy tempts you; test the word of God against temptation. If you succeed in resisting temptation, you have won the battle and saved your life.

But even if you fall, as long as you fought you get credit for fighting the good fight. As Paul states "I have fought the good fight..." (2 Timothy 4:7 NIV). You fought the good fight. Not every fight is going to be in your favor. But God will always be on your side, and so even if you fall, you land on His mercy and you can go home feeling good after a good fight. If you fail to resist temptation, it only shows that you need more practice. You have to go back and study so that the next time you fight you will succeed. You will come back even stronger. Many people don't fight—they just fall, and when you fall without a fight it shows not only your weakness and dearth of commitment but also your lack of practice. You have not read, nor prayed, nor prepared for the enemy. Are you serious or are you playing?

If you're serious you would at least try to read the word of God. When you don't prepare for the enemy, you're not interested in fighting your battle. You are an easy target for temptation. Like every profession in life, you must prepare before you engage. Jesus prepared himself in the wilderness before he engaged with the adversary and when he came out he fought with the sword of the spirit which is the word of God. Jesus was so effective with his sword that the enemy went away and left him alone. If you don't fight with the word of God the enemy will continue to use you and abuse you and tempt you because you have not a fight in you. You have to remember: bad people take advantage of other people who are weak. When weak people decide to fight back only then do they gain respect from their tormentors. When you read and take in the word of God, you can't help but tackle temptation. You can't help but throw the first punch. You can't help it because you are compelled by the Spirit of God to fight back. No longer will you be put down by the enemy or disrespected by bad people but you will be honored before God and others because you fought the good fight. When you live the word of God you will no longer be taken advantage of, or fooled, or used, or mistreated by anyone. The word of God puts a fighting spirit in you that gives you a sense of worth and power. That spirit demands you be treated with respect and walk with dignity and be embraced by love.

## *The word of God teaches, rebukes, corrects and trains*

You must believe in all scripture for all scripture is God's breath and each verse has its purpose. The purpose of the word of God is to *teach*. Once you learn the word of God, your mission is to spread it. You have to share the word of God with those with whom you come into contact. You can help someone else overcome their weaknesses with the word of God, as the word of God helped you overcome your weaknesses. You should not keep the goodness of God to yourself. The more you know the more you teach; the more you teach the more people understand the God you serve. People must know you serve a mighty God full of love and mercy.

When you spread the word of God even the enemy gets scared because the word of God challenges the talk of temptation. The talk of temptation will lead you down the road of wretchedness, but the word of God will lead you on the path of righteousness. The word of God will *rebuke* the enemy. When you rebuke the enemy you shun the ways of wickedness. You want to be in a strong position to rebuke the enemy, when he shows up, with the word of God. Rebuke is the greatest resistance to temptation because it tells the enemy face-to-face you must go. It tells the enemy he is not welcome in your space now or ever.

The word of God will *correct*. There are instructions and directions in the word of God for when you do wrong. When you go wrong, the word directs you. The word is an internal disciplinary device that is triggered to autocorrect when mistakes are made and errors are apparent. The word will hit you to correct you and punish you to right you.

The word of God *trains* you. Every follower of God must start with training. Every soldier in battle needs instructions. Training is the discipline one receives to learn what it means to walk with God. You can't walk with God unless you've been properly trained. You can't fight with the enemy unless you've been properly trained. Training is not only for you but for those who go to battle with you, as well. I wouldn't want to go into battle with anyone who hasn't been properly trained; they might hurt me and the whole company. An untrained soldier is a dangerous soldier. Those who are not properly trained can be a threat to the whole congregation. They may say words that escalate a problem rather than defuse it. They must be trained in prayer; trained in love; trained in patience; trained in faith, mercy, forgiveness, and grace. Training is an ongoing process; you must constantly and consistently train. Since you are in a battle every day, every day requires training. For the rest of your life you will be training because new advances from the enemy call for new classes from God.

All this training can be found in the scriptures. God's word takes you on a train ride—when the enemy gets on, you get off. The teaching, rebuking, correcting, training and studying are to build righteousness so you may be thoroughly equipped to do the good work of God.

# You Need Meditation in Battle (A Place to Escape)

*The depth of thought is part of the depth of life. Most of our life continues on the surface. We are enslaved by the routine of our daily lives, in work and pleasure and business and recreation. We are conquered by innumerable hazards, both good and evil. We are more driven than driving…We talk and talk and never listen to the voices speaking to our depth and from our depth…it is only when the picture that we have of ourselves breaks down completely, only when we find ourselves acting against all the expectations we had derived from that picture and only when an earthquake shakes and disrupts the surface of our self- knowledge, that we are willing to look into a deeper level of our being.*
*—Paul Tillich*

*Psalms 1:2*

You need meditation in battle. Meditation is the ability to go beyond yourself and into your spirit. Your mind, body, and soul are often used by the enemy to do his bidding; however, when you meditate on God you go deep into your spirit, where you can speak to God and God can speak to you.

Meditation helps you to lose yourself in God. You want to lose yourself in God. When you lose yourself in God, you find yourself in God's Spirit. You want to find yourself in the Holy Spirit. Meditation is the ability to absorb God and all his perfection into your own spirit so that every aspect of God becomes part of your living. To have God in your spirit is to reflect God's goodness in your life. God's goodness is His love, grace, mercy, peace, patience, joy, and forgiveness.

When you meditate on God and all His goodness, this very meditation becomes a defense against the enemy's attacks. The enemy attacks us with the opposite of God's goodness. In other words, when God gives us love, the enemy attacks us with hate. When God gives us peace, the enemy attacks us with pain. When God gives us patience, the enemy attacks us with anger. Even when God pardons our transgressions, the enemy attacks us with guilt. Yet when you build up your defense, the enemy's attack becomes powerless and meaningless. Our goal as men and women of God is to build up our defense so that we can resist the enemy's attacks against His goodness. Meditation is for real; it brings out the goodness of God and the goodness of God brings out the best in you. You become kinder, gentler, more loving, more forgiving, and more powerful to fight against your opposition. The more we meditate, the more God is in us and with us. The more God is in you, the less the enemy throws at you, because if God is for you, who can win against you? God within you is stronger than the enemy coming at you.

Meditation is a deep concentration that shifts your attention from your suffering to your overcoming. Many people suffer from anxiety, stress, and trauma, and these aberrations can cause serious unhappiness in life. The enemy loves that lives are disrupted and distracted because of abnormalities; however, meditation digs into your spirit to pull out peace and happiness to confront disturbances and shift your attention. With meditation, you focus on peace to replace anxiety and stress and you concentrate on joy to subdue and control trauma. Meditation makes you think of peaceful people, places, and times that bring happiness to your life. Meditation brings calm and control to your existence. Meditation is like medicine; it gets into your spirit to heal your mind, body, and soul. It releases you from any abnormalities so you can focus on God's glory, beauty, and wonder in your life.

When David's soul was troubled he sought the beauty of the Lord, "One thing have I desired of the Lord, that will I seek after; that I may dwell in the house of the Lord all the days of my life, *to behold the beauty* of the Lord, and to enquire in his temple" (Psalm 27:4 KJV).

Meditation is a process that puts you in a different, more excellent state of being. It is a place of escape, a getaway, a retreat. One thing David did regularly was meditate on God's goodness even in the midst of his actual battles. Meditation pulled him away from the battle by putting him in a different state of mind. Most battles in our lives are fraught with tension and worry which can result in serious mental and emotional disturbances. What David did was meditate on the goodness of God day and night, "But his delight is in the law of the Lord; and in his law does he meditate day and night" (Psalms 1:2 KJV). The law of the Lord was God's goodness; His peace, joy, holiness and righteous acts. Once David meditated on the goodness, he then entered into the goodness. In Psalms 23 David says, "He maketh me to lie down in green pastures: he leadeth me besides the still waters. He restoreth my soul: he leadeth me in the path of righteousness for his name's sake." (Psalm 23:2-3 KJV). Meditation actually brings you into the very goodness that you are seeking. It is a place to escape all the madness, sadness and stress of life. Some people don't have the time or the means to go on long vacations, relax on a beach or sit on a mountain. However meditation brings you to the place of peace and calm. David sought peace, calm and righteousness. And God pulled his mind and emotions into a place of escape by *lying him down in green pastures, leading him besides the still waters, restoring his soul and leading him in the path of righteousness.* David actually became the goodness that he meditated on and was able to conquer fear, worry and enemies.

If you are in a battle against worry, fear and anxiety you want to go into battle with peace, calm and confidence. In order to go in with the goodness of God you must first meditate on it. Meditate on peace. Meditate on joy. Meditate on calm. It will put your mind and soul at ease. When you meditate you replace what's bothering you with what strengthens you. Once you meditate on it, you then enter into it. When you enter into it, you lose yourself in the very goodness, *peace, joy, love,* that you are seeking. You don't exit until you feel like the goodness that you are seeking is actually in your spirit. You don't leave until you feel at peace, at ease; until you feel happy. You will know when you feel it because what was disturbing you will no longer be a distractor in your life. In other words, if you were scared before you meditated you don't come out until you feel confident and calm in your spirit. Once you have it in your spirit, you then become the very goodness that God has made possible for your battle in life. When you actually become the goodness your mind is clearer. When your mind is clearer your focus is better. When your focus is better you speak clearer and handle situations better.

Many people stumble over their words and mumble their words because they are not focused, they don't think clearly before they speak. The enemy loves a tumbler because he knows you are not focused in your battle. Fear and worry are paralyzers. When you have to present or speak at a meeting or defend a client you want to be clear. You want to be unafraid and confident. Mediation builds up calm and confidence in your spirit that is reflected in your presence.

God's word tells of His perfection. God's word tells of all His goodness toward us. When we meditate on God's word, we are taking all of God's goodness into our spirit, so that what is in God's word is not only in us but *is us.*

We want to be doers of the word and not hearers only. Many people separate themselves from what they know of God and who they are in God. Many people know the word of God and know the goodness of God but have not become the word or the goodness of what they know. In order for God's word to be real in your life you have to become it. When you meditate you actually become the goodness of God. You become the peace and the joy and the love that God puts into your spirit. When people see you they should see the manifestation of God's peace. They should be able to say that you are a man or a woman of grace. They should be able to say you are a person of love and happiness because you demonstrate God's goodness in your actions. You have actually become the goodness that you speak of. The manifestation of God's goodness makes you a real representative of the God you serve.

When you meditate on God's word, the word of God goes from your head to your heart to your spirit. When the word of God is in your spirit, it becomes your very existence. With the word of God in us, we begin to live consciously for Him. The word of God not only reminds us of His will but also guides us away from the enemy's wishes. Meditating on the word becomes a compass for our lives. It leads us away from temptation and toward God's blessings. It turns us away from the ungodly, away from the ways of the wicked, and away from the seat of the scornful.

Meditation makes it a delight, a joy, to think on the word of the Lord both day and night. When you meditate on the word of God day and night you are building up such a resistance against temptation that your living becomes an example for others. You are working on living totally for God, and the more you live totally for God, the more people will get the message and respect your new life.

Many people don't get respect from others in their living for God because they are inconsistent. They're living contradictions, wavering between good and evil, God and the enemy. They fall easily into temptation. They pray for the sick but complain when they're sick. They can shake hands with the saints while cussing with the sinners. They can praise God with one tongue and lie to people with the same tongue. They can go to worship in the morning and live dangerously at night.

Of course this may represent an internal struggle but those who have not meditated on the word of God are not struggling but playing. They have no consciousness of or conviction for God. They go to God but do not necessarily live for God. When you live in between God and the enemy your life is too much of a paradox for anyone to appreciate and follow. It's easy to recognize people who are all evil or all good. It's easy to stay away from people you know who are no good. But wolves in sheep clothing can fool you. People who are half-good and half-evil can't be trusted. They will befriend you only to shun you. They will smile in your face and stab you in your back. When people can't trust you they don't respect you. When they don't respect you as a person of God, they turn away from God.

Meditation challenges the contradictions and eliminates the enigmas so that you will live fully for God. When you live fully for God, people will respect you because they will see that even if you fall you are trying, even if you roam you are conscious, and even if you do wrong you have conviction.

Meditation offers conviction because the spirit is troubled when temptation enters in and the enemy breaks down your other defenses. When temptation breaks down your defense, it means the enemy can increase his attacks against your existence. The enemy has a way of sending in more potent demons to challenge your living especially when you're trying to beat your weakness. The enemy will send in double your pleasure from the single pleasure to tempt you and break down your doors. In other words, if the enemy knows that your weakness is food, he will make food available in multiple ways through multiple people and places to tempt you and make you fall. If that does not work he'll send in double your trouble to break down your spirit. If that doesn't work the enemy will send in triple your pleasure and triple your trouble to tempt you and desecrate you at the same time. The enemy wants to break down your walls, and so he will send in a barrage of money, sex, drugs, women, men, power, sadness, loneliness, sickness and every kind of grenade he can think of to destroy you.

Such attacks require greater meditation.

The more you meditate, the more holy you become, the more defense and power you build up. When you meditate, it pushes the spirit of God into you and the enemy out of you. And you're going to need a heavy push from God's spirit to deal with the triple-threat that's coming at you. Another reason why you have to meditate day and night is because the enemy will tempt you day and night. The enemy is persistent. His aim is to attack your spirit, drag you to your grave and leave you dying in your mess.

But meditation is God's way of saying *I am with you; I will never leave you nor forsake you; I am stronger than your enemy; I am more powerful than temptation.* When you meditate, God's voice echoes throughout your mind, body, and soul and gives you power.

## *Meditate on God's power, love, hope, forgiveness, peace and truth*

You have to meditate on God's *power.* We serve a powerful God. There is no one that can compare or compete with God. Once you get God in your spirit you receive power. And this power can knock down doors and break down walls the enemy is hiding behind in your life. The bible says "God has not given us the spirit of fear; but of power, and of love, and of a sound mind" (2 Timothy 1:7). God's power gets into secret and secluded places to destroy fear, worry and lies to bring love and calm to your life. You can't hide any wrongs from God. Put His power in your spirit. God's power can defeat the triple threat that the enemy throws at you. God is a God of power, might, and strength. His power can overcome any temptation. His might can conquer any defilement. His strength can prevent any fall. You can't go wrong with God. Literally, you cannot go wrong. God's power helps you to stand up rather than submit to your weakness. You have to learn to stand up and face your enemy and stop running and hiding like a coward. God's power gives you courage. Courage to face and fight your adversary. God is a God of righteousness that keeps you on the right path, and anything wrong must be challenged. Meditation is a cleansing mechanism for our spirits; the more evil we push out, the more God we put in.

You have to meditate on God's *love* because the enemy's hate is real. You can't truly love until you have God because the scriptures tell us God is love. Many people claim to have been hurt by love, but in fact, love does not hurt; hate hurts, and the enemy will use hate to hurt love.

God's love does not hurt; it comforts. As a result of being hurt, many people give up on love. And the enemy wins when you give up on love because when you give up on love, you give up on God. Love is the essence of God's being in your life. If you forfeit love, you lose God and when you lose God you lose the battle. You must go into battle with love not hate.

When you meditate, you seek to restore God's love into your life so that even if you've been hurt you can still love. When you meditate love goes deep into your spirit, and when love is in the spirit no one and nothing can take it away. God's love is resilient. It gets bruised, assaulted, knocked down, and loves again. God's love is everlasting. It gets tired, drained, and hurt, but it never runs out.

When you have the love of God you don't mind serving others. God's love shows itself to everyone. It does not discriminate. It should be no surprise that God's love even shows itself to His enemies. God's love prays for His enemies. God's love is good to those who hate Him and helps those who cuss Him. This is serious love and may seem stupid at first glance. How can anyone love someone who hurts them and hates them? God's love continues to love even when the enemy attacks because God's love is not controlled by the enemy's attacks; God's love is controlled by God. If God's love stopped just because the enemy attacked, then that would mean that the enemy controls God's love, and if the enemy controls God's love, the enemy controls God.

Not!

God's love remains constant because God is love and God's love is stronger than the enemy's hate. In other words, the enemy's attacks are not strong enough to affect God or God's people. The enemy's attacks cannot and should not move God's people away from God's love. This is not just your love. When you meditate you receive God's love which is stronger than your love and the enemy's hate. God's love is a weapon in battle. It is a shield that keeps your character intact. It is a safeguard that helps you maintain your integrity and prevents you from being like the enemy. Most people hate because other people hate them. Most people insult because other people insult them. Most people do evil because other people do evil to them. We have become a people of retaliation. When you hate, insult, and do evil because of other people, you are controlled by other people and not by God; therefore, God is not truly in you. Love is constant so that God's light shines in darkness.

Those who hurt you will be hurt by their own hate. Those who insult you will be insulted by their own insults because they won't understand why you are still standing while they're attacking. The bible says "God is not mocked, you reap what you sow" (Galatians 6:7) When you sow hate you will reap hate. When you sow love, you will reap love. People won't understand why you are kind and considerate while they're cold and uncontrolled. Here again, your haters are hurt by their own attacks because people can't be happy when they're cold and out of control.

God's love won't allow their attacks to overcome you as long as you keep on loving them. And loving them does not mean allowing them to take advantage of your kindness or exploit your righteousness. Loving them mean remaining committed to God's will while not permitting them to control your actions or move you from God's goodness. When you hate back it means they control you, when you love back it means God is in you.

If you keep on loving them they'll get what they deserve. They'll fall in the hole they dug for you. They'll get caught in their own traps, and become the victims of their own deceit. They will trip on their own words, be confronted by their own conscience, and be hit by their own attacks. God's love is not romantic; it is protective, just like any mother with her child. God's love strikes and blocks and pushes and knocks and is capable of killing off all attacks. All you have to do is meditate on God's love and God will handle the battle.

The enemy would love to abolish love because when love is vanquished relationships between people are destroyed. If you meditate on the word of God you will see that love for neighbors is encouraged. As a matter of fact, it is one of the central laws in the word of God. The enemy's goal is to destroy neighborly love because neighborly love keeps people in communion with each other. It keeps people in congregation with one another. It keeps people in marriage, family, community, and work with one another. And when God's love resonates it keeps people in harmony with one another. God is a God of peace not chaos.

But the enemy does not like God's community or harmony. The enemy loves division and dissention, conflict and arguing, and will plant the seed of temptation in order to destroy good relations between God's people. The sad thing is, it's not hard for the enemy to find someone to start a conflict in God's community because there are a lot of weak people in God's army. And the enemy just needs one weakling to cause chaos. The enemy rejoices when people who are supposed to be godly turn nasty.

But just like the enemy needs one to cause fraction, God needs one to protect unity. It is good when the people of God live in unity. The person who has been meditating on the love of God, on the peace of God, on the grace of God, and on the power of God will be the one who God uses to beat the enemy and keep His community together. Sometimes all it takes is one praying person to keep the family together. Sometimes all it takes is one loving person to keep the church united and the community together. When you have been meditating on God's goodness, God strengthens you not only for your own battle but also for your neighbors' fight against the enemy.

God needs leaders, and leaders must show that they are strong enough to fight temptation for themselves and show others the way, truth and light. God needs leaders that are strong enough to show Him mighty and strong against temptation. God needs leaders to lead others to battle against arguing, dissention and hate. God needs leaders to meditate on His word day and night.

The reason why it is easy to cause enmity in God's community is because many of God's people don't love themselves. Loving yourself is an important command because it shows a connection with God. We are made in God's image, after his likeness, so if we don't love ourselves we don't love God who made us. If we don't love God who made us, how can we live in peace and harmony with ourselves and others? If we don't love ourselves, then we will only be the cause of conflict and confusion. The enemy uses our lack of love for self to destroy our love for others, our feelings for life and our relationships with God. The lack of love for self can result in suicide, homicide, and deviant and promiscuous behavior. Such lack of love for self can easily be passed down to children and other family members. Meditation on the love of God can build up love of self.

When you think about the goodness of God and all that God has done in your life, how can you not love yourself? God's mercy forgave you; God's protection saved you from dangers seen and unseen. God loved you when others dumped you and you denied yourself. God's grace allowed you to step into another day when you could've or should've slipped into disgrace and the grave. God's love for us is stronger than our love for ourselves. God proves it by waking us every morning. If you feel like you don't have love for self, meditate on God's love for you and you will know that He loves you enough to keep you. If He loves you enough to keep you, the least you can do is love yourself for Him.

I understand that some people may not love themselves because of what other people have said and done. You may not love yourself because other people have been mean and cruel in their wording and in their treatment of you. You may have been called really bad and disgusting names by other people—stupid, dumb, no good, lazy, ugly, et cetera. You may even believe the names you've been called. You may have been treated horribly by other people—been sexually abused, violated, molested, cheated on, lied to, physically abused, abandoned, et cetera. This may have wrecked your life and caused you to do things that are dirty, disgusting, and wrong.

But this is where you must meditate on God's goodness. You must go into battle against every wrong that you've been called and encountered with the goodness of God. God's goodness can beat down all the badness that has been done to you. Start by listing each wrong in your life that holds you hostage and then counter it with God's love to keep you, God's power to free you, God's beauty to hold you and God's protection to bring you through it all. Then leave all the wrong behind, shut the door and walk in the spirit and the freedom of God's Goodness. God's goodness can free you from all the filth you've been called and cleanse you from all the wrongs you've endured. When God cleans you, you get a new attitude about self and life. You go from feeling disgusting and dirty to feeling fresh and renewed. You go from feeling sad to feeling good. Meditate on God's goodness it will make you feel and look good.

God's goodness takes you from hopeless to hopeful. You must meditate on God's *hope* for your life. Hope is a powerful tool that gives meaning and beauty to your life. Nothing makes you feel better than when you have hope. Hope easily beats despair. You must go into battle with hope. When you have hope you wake up looking forward to another day and every day should make you feel good because you have an opportunity to make things better than the day before. God allowed you to see another day. God sees you as precious; God makes you feel special. Just the fact that God kept you when others left you should make you feel exceptional. You could have died from all the stuff you've done and the stuff that has been done to you but God kept you another day. The fact that God kept you alive should give you zest and zeal for a great future.

God not only cleans you and loves you but gives you *forgiveness*. When you go into battle with forgiveness you can beat hate, anger, and shame that you may feel toward others. Forgiveness must not only be a word that you use but also a tool that you carry. In other words, meditation will put forgiveness in you to carve out any hate, feelings of sorrow, lack of love, or memory you carry about your victimization. Meditating on God's love uplifts your feelings and heals your emotions. When you meditate you make a conscious decision to leave behind your victimization. Your victimization is no longer your enemy because God's love is your friend. And your friend is stronger than your enemy. You are loved. Meditating steps in and removes all feelings of guilt and shame.

It erases bad memories that haunt you and trauma that taunts you and replaces it with thoughts that celebrate your living and overcoming. You are an overcomer! You are more than a conqueror! Celebrate!

You have to remember, unforgiveness hurts the victim more than it does the perpetrator. You are the victim of cruel and malicious acts but you don't want to live in your victimization, you want to live in God's goodness. God's goodness heals and delivers. God's love frees and protects. You are under God's protection and have been freed from your victimization. You want to be free from the violations against you and the penalty that haunts you. Forgiveness will free you and bring peace to your life. Meditate on God's freedom because who God sets free is free indeed.

You need peace in your life. Meditate on God's *peace* for your life. Peace brings calm from the noise and healing from the pain. Why should you have to suffer because of other people's wrongs and your own negative emotions? That's a double whammy. Meditation helps you to go beyond yourself and into God's spirit. As stated, the self is prone to weakness and submission to temptation and will keep you drowning in your victimization, hurting from your past and trauma-tized from incidents. Meditation moves beyond the self, digs into the spirit and pulls you to safety. You are safe now! You may have been a victim in the past but you are safe now! You've been rescued by the love of God. You are free from your past and from yourself because of peace. Peace helps you to focus on your now and not on your perpetrator or prior life.

This can also work for the person who has been the perpetrator of cruel and malicious acts upon others. There are many people in prison (either in an actual cell behind bars or in a mental state behind tears) who are living in deep regret for something they did to someone else. They have killed, raped, robbed, assaulted, and committed all kinds of verbal and physical violence against people. Some are reaping what they sow. But God is a God of mercy and forgiveness for everyone, the victim and the perpetrator. The bible says "He causes his sun to rise on

the evil and the good, and sends rain on the righteous and the unrigh-
teous" (Matthew 5:45 NIV). If you have done wrong to anyone and are
feeling remorseful for what you've done, you have to meditate on God's
forgiveness and mercy. Forgiveness will free you from the wrong you've
committed and mercy will pardon you from its penalty, bringing peace
to your life. You don't want to live in regret, you want to repent and live
in God's perfect peace. When you live in perfect peace it can free you
no matter where you are; whether you are in prison, in isolation or in
the hospital.

When you seek forgiveness and mercy, God gives it freely. God
knows your heart. You can't fool God with many words; God knows
your feelings and your spirit. When you meditate on love, forgiveness,
and mercy, God listens because this meditation leads to a place where
God can hear and communicate.

The bible says "God is a Spirit and they that worship him must
worship him in spirit and in truth" (John 4:24). When you meditate
on God's *truth* God's Spirit will tell you the truth about yourself. Many
people don't like to hear the truth about them self. Many people believe
they have no problems with sinning and are not struggling with temptation. Many people are good at pointing out other people's sins but
can't see the sin in themselves. But you have to first take the plank out
of your eye and you will see clearly to remove it from someone else's eyes
(Matthew 7:5). In other words, you have to confess and correct your
wrongs before you criticize and correct other people's mistakes. Many
people believe just because they're not doing the specific wrong others
are doing they don't have a problem with evil. They're living a lie. And
the enemy loves a denier.

The only way to beat a lie is with the truth. Meditation helps you
reveal the truth about yourself. If you are suffering with selfishness and
stubbornness and deceit it will be revealed if you meditate on God's
truth. God does not tell you the truth to hurt you but rather to better
you. The enemy makes you believe you have no flaws. But God reveals
your flaws to strengthen you against temptation. Again, everybody is

struggling against something and even if it's not to the degree of others, it's still a weakness that must be confronted. God will reveal your wrongs so that you can fight the enemy and live for God. God will tell you the truth about yourself, even if you don't want to hear it. It is up to you to confront, and hopefully to correct, the wrong and evict the enemy from your life. When the truth moves from your head to your heart to your spirit, God hears you loud and clear. That is why you must meditate day and night—because you're moving the goodness of God into a place that the enemy can't touch.

The enemy can mess with your mind, the enemy can mess with your heart, but once you put the word of God in your spirit, it is in a lock box. It is sealed. It becomes part of your living. And your living will free your mind and clean your heart. When God's goodness is your very existence you live it day and night. You go to sleep *with* God, you wake up *with* God, you walk the streets *with* God, you go to work *with* God, you get married *with* God. You battle *with* God. Everything you do is *with* God.

This meditation can be done in many different ways from singing and dancing to painting and poetry. Some people are very artistic and can use their creativity to meditate on God's goodness. Art is an expression of the gift of God and the gift of God should be used to enter into God. David used song and dance to express the goodness of God. Most of the Psalms written in the bible are a result of David's meditation upon God. When you use the gift of God to express God's goodness, flesh no longer has control over your life but you control your flesh for life and live happy.

# You Need Fasting in Battle
## (A Partner)

*When all is said and done, the life of faith is nothing if not an unending struggle of the spirit with every available weapon against the flesh. How is it possible to live the life of faith when we grow weary of prayer, when we lose our taste for reading the Bible, and when sleep, food and sensuality deprive us of the joy of communion with God?*
—*Dietrich Bonhoeffer*

## Matthew 6:16

You need fasting to battle temptation. Fasting is the ability to deny self and seek God. Fasting tames the flesh and empowers the spirit. Fasting is possibly the most spiritually effective yet the most physically difficult tool to use because it involves sacrifice. When you sacrifice you give up stuff you enjoy. You cut off things that feel good, look good and taste good. Fasting is so challenging because you are actually fighting yourself to get to God. You are fighting your flesh to get to God's spirit.

Most people want to get to God but they don't want to give up the flesh. Everybody wants to go to heaven but nobody wants to die.

The enemy uses the flesh to carry out his mission of evil. When we deny the flesh we take the weapon out of the enemy's hands and put ourselves back in God's care. To be in God's care is to *know* that God will take care of you.

But the flesh is often used as the antithesis of God's purpose. The spirit is willing but the flesh is weak. Weak flesh causes havoc in our lives. Weak flesh increases the enemy's ability to lure the body into temptation. The body seeks satisfaction and overindulgence in its greed. The body wants glamour, pleasure, fame, and an abundance of food. Satisfying the flesh can get you into a lot of trouble. The enemy knows what the body wants and will provide all the desires to keep flesh under control. When you are under the enemy's control you are constantly sinning against God. The enemy will use your flesh to keep you away from God because the enemy knows that if you reach God, God will save you from the flesh. When the enemy lures your body he puts you at odds with God's spiritual purpose for your life. When the spirit and flesh are at odds, a battle rages inside you. In order for the spirit of God to win the battle you need something to go into battle with and the best weapon to take into battle is fasting. Fasting helps you to get closer to God's spirit. When you get closer to God's spirit you have a friend, a partner, a supplier in battle. When the flesh kicks out the spirit of God kicks in.

Fasting is for real; it actually cuts down the flesh so that you can get closer to God. Many people are afraid of fasting because it infringes upon their desires and can be difficult to carry out. Most people think of fasting as a physical act rather than a spiritual one, and as long as they think of it as a physical act they will never conquer the flesh.

If you really want to tackle the enemy you must think of fasting as a spiritual action. In other words, don't start with the premise *I'm giving up something*; instead, start with the premise *I'm gaining something*. If you think of fasting as giving up food, then your mind and body will be on the food. If your mind is on the food, then how can you conquer the flesh? Starting with the flesh is a losing proposition.

However, if you think of fasting as gaining something, you start with a winning proposal. When you start with this winning proposal you will *gain* a closer relationship with God. You will *gain* victory over the enemy. You will *gain* a new attitude, mind, body, and soul. When you think of gaining from fasting it will make you more determined and less afraid to tackle the flesh. When you think you will gain a greater relationship with God along with his blessings, you will be more determined to deny the flesh. In order to gain what God has for you, you have to go deeper: Deep calls to deep. The deeper you go, the more flesh you deny. The more flesh you deny, the more enemy you destroy. You have to understand the enemy seeks to clog your life with desires that will take you away from God, and with the abundance of material it is not hard to overindulge in this world. The flesh can be easily manipulated by powerful agents of captivity, from food to clothes to shopping to technology to sex and so much more that it's hard to see God in the crowd. It's hard to hear God in the noise. It's hard to find God when you're lost in the world. The enemy puts up such a buffer between us and God that it's going to take a miracle to tear down the walls and get closer to God. When you fast you tear down walls that separate you from God. When you fast you get less static and better communication with God. Fasting breaks down the buffer and removes the interruption of the world that blocks our connection with God.

Fasting cuts at the enemy and denies the flesh to give you a line of communication with God. When you have a connection with God you begin to see the light of a new day after living in darkness for so long. Fasting actually gives you control over your life. You are no longer controlled by the enemy. You are no longer controlled by the flesh. Remember, the enemy seeks to control you by giving you the desires of the flesh. Once you reject the enemy's advances, you actually *gain* control over your life. When you have control over your life you feel better and look better because you are with God. And when you are with God you get all that God has to resist the desires of the flesh.

Fulfilling the desires of the flesh can leave you feeling bad and looking sad after you've overindulged with food. Obesity is a big problem for many people. You must have discipline to battle obesity. Fasting gives you discipline and discipline controls your consumption. Once you control your eating, you control your life. Once you learn to tame the flesh you *gain* a healthy and happy lifestyle. When your lifestyle is different, you live in moderation rather than in excess. Excess is an expression of greed. Greed is what the enemy uses to rob us of our savings and steal our spiritual connection. When you are greedy not only are you selfish but you are wasteful and have little regard for others which makes you sinful. You need moderation to battle excess and greed. Fasting will keep you in moderation because it is an agent of freedom against captivity. That's right: Fasting frees you from the hands of the enemy. You now have the freedom to choose what and when you will eat or not eat, where you will go or not go, and what you will do or not do in your new lifestyle.

Prior to fasting you were totally controlled by the flesh, which means you were not free to choose between right and wrong, between moderation and greed. The enemy can have such control over your life that he takes away your freedom to choose, and when you have no freedom to choose you are locked in the flesh of death. But once you break out of the enemy's captivity, you are free to seek God for life and live more happily.

You need a breakthrough, and fasting gives you the breakthrough you need to see God's power and receive God's blessings. Once you break through the flesh you go deeper into God and get access to blessings and answers. It's like going deep into the earth until you find water, oil, or gold. When you break through the flesh, you get to the living water, the oil of anointment, and you will come forth as gold. God's breakthrough is powerful. When you get a breakthrough from God you hear the answer to your inquiry. You receive the blessings you've been looking for, and doors begin to open.

The enemy can have you in such confinement that you don't seek God, ask God, or knock on God's door. The enemy knows once we seek the kingdom of God and his righteousness all things will be given. Fasting will show you all that the flesh was hiding from you. Fasting will show you how the enemy was trying to block your blessings. The reason the enemy used the flesh was because he knew it was a great deterrent; he knows what's behind closed doors. The enemy knows God has happiness for you behind those walls. The enemy knew that if he could just keep you over eating and drinking and sexing and texting you would never see God's blessings. God has an answer to your problem. God has happiness for your sadness. God has riches for your poverty. God has someone for your loneliness. Once you break through the flesh you will see that your life can be so much happier.

## Three, Ten, Forty day fast

Fasting increases your partnership with God and God's will for your life. When you read the scriptures you see that when Esther fasts for three days she got a breakthrough in her spirit which gave her boldness and confidence. She not only got boldness and confidence but answers to her questions and protection from her enemies. God was so good that she saw her enemy fall and her people rise. Fasting will give you boldness and confidence to battle weakness and uncertainty. Esther wanted an immediate change in her circumstances. She had a particular issue she needed God to resolve.

If you have a particular issue that you want God to answer, you may need a three-day fast. A three-day fast is a total commitment with a total focus on the issue at hand. You must identify the issue and then fast and pray. When you specify the problem and fast, you are giving the issue to God. When you give the issue to God it is no longer your issue but God's to answer. Your fasting keeps you waiting on the answer rather than worrying about the issue. Esther waits on the answer and when she receives the answer, she is able to boldly confront the issue. You can't confront the issue unless you first get an answer from God.

If you deal with the issue without God you will lose the battle. The enemy would love for you to go into battle without God. Some people move so impetuously. When you go into battle without God the flesh begins to say things to escalate the problem rather than defuse it. You have to remember: Flesh responds evil for evil and insult for insult.

You need fasting to keep the flesh in check so that it does not resort to evil. When you fast and pray you are asking God to control your actions and monitor your speech. You don't need to respond to everything thrown at you from the enemy; that just shows a lack of faith. You need self-control. Self-control will tackle obnoxious, impatient and self-indulging behavior.

When you fast, God controls your tongue so that the flesh does not get you into more trouble. When you fast, God subdues your actions so that you do not respond in a mean and malicious and violent manner that escalates the problem. The reason why many relationships are so strained is because the enemy tempts us to respond negatively to every little action and insult thrown at us. You must learn that the enemy's plan is to have us kill each other off by the things we do and say. Fast and pray so that you do not fall into the enemy's trap. Fasting will help you live with people more peacefully and lovingly.

When you read the scripture you see that when Daniel fasts for ten days he becomes healthier and better-nourished than all others. Daniel gains a better appearance and feeling. There is something about fasting that makes you look good and feel great. When you look good and feel great it is a reflection of God. God does not want his people to look busted and feel bad when they fast. The scriptures states "when you fast do not look somber" (Matthew 5:16). The idea that you are releasing toxins from your flesh and sins from your spirit should make you feel healthier and look better. Purging is a process that takes time to cleanse infestations. You not only want to be forgiven; you also want to be cleansed. Forgiveness eliminates the sin, cleansing washes the sinner. When you are cleansed you no longer walk around with the dirt of your past. You walk around with the hope of your future. You should walk easier because you are not weighed down by the poisons in your flesh.

If you want to be healthier and feel better you may need a ten-day fast. If the flesh is a burden and life is weighing you down, you may want to withdraw from meat for ten days. Daniel's fast consists of vegetables and water, which showed he not only had regard for the spirit but also for the body. When you fast you become conscious of what goes into your body. You must take care of your body. The enemy doesn't care about your body. He just uses and abuses it, but you must care for it.

The enemy uses the body but so does God. The body is God's temple and should be used to carry out God's will. God needs a clean and healthy body to carry out his will. Fasting gives you respect for your body and for your health. When you have respect for your health you keep the body in shape. You exercise daily and eat healthily. You cleanse the body of anything that might cause its destruction, such as smoking, overdrinking, or drug use. When you have regard for your body, not just anything or anybody can enter in; it is safeguarded for the holy; it is preserved for the deserving. The temple of God is sacred and to be held with the utmost honor and respect. It is not to be used for unholy pleasure or lustful fascination; it is to be robed royally and to be cherished and loved.

The enemy would love for you to desecrate and disrespect your body because it opens the door to disease and damnation. You want to do all you can to protect your body, and the best way to protect the body is to fast and pray. Fasting keeps the body regal and the face glowing with God's glory. When you glow with the glory of God you can rely on your own compliments. You can tell yourself you look good. You don't need compliments from anyone else to feel good because the glow of God speaks for itself. Some folks are always waiting on other people's praises, but when you have fasted and prayed God has already spoken to you about yourself and you should know how good you look because God is good.

When you read the word of God you will see that Jesus fasts for forty days. When Jesus fasts for forty days, He comes out ready for a big battle against the enemy. Jesus' fast made Him powerful and knowledgeable. Jesus had the power to resist temptation and the knowledge to see through the enemy's tricks. The enemy's first temptation for Jesus is something to eat. The enemy offers Jesus bread. The enemy is watching you while you're fasting to see if you come out powerful enough to resist temptation and knowledgeable to recognize his tricks.

The enemy will tempt you to see if you are the same or changed as a result of fasting. If you are the same, you will prove that you were not serious about your fast and will be put to shame by the enemy. The enemy will continue to mess with you and eventually ruin your life. If you have changed you will resist temptation and show that your lifestyle is no longer the same.

When you fast for a lengthy period of time it shows that you want to make a lifestyle change. You are not only interested in a particular issue or health and appearance but a new life. You want to change the way you were living and acting to be more committed in the life of Christ. Jesus' fast becomes the paradigm for a lifestyle change. Some people fast and then after the fast pick up the same old habits that they had before the fast. But the forty day fast changes your life forever so that you don't go back to that which you're fasting from. If you are fasting from chicken because you feel it is causing health and spiritual issues because you can't control yourself when you see it, then fasting becomes a way to stop eating chicken for good so that your body and soul can be at peace. If you are fasting from cussing because you can't seem to stop swearing every time you speak, then after a forty day fast you should be able to put away cussing forever. A forty day fast is a serious makeover of your body, mind, and soul. You won't be able to think the same or feel the same after this makeover because God would have extremely worked on you. Like a potter to clay you are being molded and made from the inside out. God is creating in you a clean heart and right spirit.

Some people believe that fasting only affects the body; but a real fast affects: body, mind, heart and soul. When you fast you not only rid the body of immoralities but seek to free the mind of impurities, the heart of insecurities and the soul of unhappiness. The forty day fast not only keeps your body from dishonest engagements, but keeps your mouth from unwholesome conversations and your mind from unholy thoughts. A forty day fast keeps your heart from anything or anyone that may hurt it or break it; like certain people. It keeps your soul from anything or anyone that may disturb it or depress it; like certain unhappy instances and places. A forty day fast cleanses from the inside out so that you come forth totally new.

An earnest fast puts you in a serious battle against the enemy. The enemy does not want you to change your life. The enemy wants you to continue on the path of destruction. The enemy has a hard time with a three-day fast that put him under your foot and turns your circumstances to your favor. The enemy has a hard time with a ten-day fast that makes you look and feel better. Now, if the enemy has to deal with a forty-day fast, it will not only change your circumstances and make you look and feel better but will turn your whole life around from the inside out and put you in a place that is secure, sincere and happy.

With a 40 day fast you actually become more loving of yourself and of others. You actually see the hope that you've been waiting for. You can no longer tolerate falling to temptation. It becomes a distraction to your goals and disturbance to your soul. You can no longer live with certain vices. You no longer want to live desperately or recklessly but faithfully and loyally to yourself and others. You don't want to live a lie but your new life demands the truth whether people like it or not; whether people agree with it or not. You are who you are in God and you won't allow anyone, any longer, to dictate who you should be or what you should be as long as you are living righteously and not intentionally hurting anybody. A lifestyle change opens the door to freedom and happiness.

After a 40 day fast you will have built up enough resistance to confront and even dismiss your weakness. Many people live running or hiding from their temptation. They turn around or head in another direction when they see their weakness coming. I know a man whose weakness was women and after he fasted and prayed to end his weakness, his method was to run every time he saw a woman so he could avoid temptation. That's not resisting, that's running and it shows nothing came of your fasting except running faster. You can't run or hide from your weakness because sooner or later it's going to catch up to you. Running, turning or hiding does not show that God is working in your life or that fasting is effective.

When you have fasted to end temptation and built up enough resistance you should be able to face your former weakness with confidence and dismiss it with authority. It should no longer be a problem in your life. You want to be at a party and see liquor and dismiss it as if it were never a problem. You want to watch television with sex in it and dismiss lust from your mind as if it were never a bother. You want to be at a bakery and not have to worry about falling to temptation and eating every cake in the place. You can't prove God's power if you don't confront and dismiss your former enemy. Jesus came out of his forty day fast looking the enemy dead in the eye and dismissing him with boldness and certainty. When you have fasted for forty days you should be able to boldly dismiss the enemy and render his tactics ineffective. What once was your weakness is no longer your problem so don't run or hide, confront and dismiss.

Your new lifestyle will automatically align you with new people and disengage you from old friends. Some people you will leave and other people will leave you. The transition won't be easy but it will be worth it. Whatever you do, don't turn back. Keep going with the flow of your fast. It will take you through sickness and sadness to lead you to safety and happiness. You will go through the valley, lose friends and family but become a better person that attracts a different standard and quality of people. After a while the old life will be a distant memory and the new life will be a great reality. As with Jesus, you will become more powerful and knowledgeable after a forty day fast. Every day of the fast you will get stronger and smarter. Every day of the fast you build up resistance and determination to go all the way. Even if you fall, you get up and walk on. Every day of the fast you will become a better person. You want to be a better person. You want to be a humble person. You want to be a kind person. You want to be considerate and self-controlled. When you are new and better, you will attract new and better people. Whatever you are is what you will attract; *you reap what you sow.*

The forty day fast will free you from your past. As stated the past is a great deterrent and disturbance to many people's progress. Many people are haunted by mistakes and regrets from their past. You don't want to live with regrets of your former life or mistakes of things you've done before your transformation. What is done is done. Your new self creates a better life that brings you into a place of peace and reconciliation. Peace and reconciliation give you something to battle with against mistakes and regrets. Peace will put your soul at ease from mistakes you've made and reconciliation will put you in a place of contentment that allows you to admit your faults and move on. You don't want to be held hostage by faults or persecuted by mistakes. It does nothing but hold you back from your future happiness.

With a forty-day fast "Thou shalt not be afraid of the terror by night; nor for the arrow that flieth by day; nor for the pestilence that walketh in darkness; nor for the destruction that wasteth at noonday; a thousand shall fall at thy side, and ten thousand at thy right hand; but it shall not come nigh thee. Only with thine eyes shalt thy behold and see the reward of the wicked" (Psalms 91:5-8 KJV).

Once you change your life you are bringing in spiritual possessions that dictate your direction. No longer will the enemy control your footsteps nor tempt you easily and cause havoc in your life. You are changed! You are changed! You are changed!

A lifestyle change means new friends, new surroundings, new communion and new relationships all because there is a new you.

## Fasting with praying, scripture, meditating and faith go hand in hand

And I must emphasize that *fasting and praying* go hand-in-hand. If you fast without praying, you are dieting rather than communing. You want to commune with God during your fast. You want to talk to God about strength to continue your fast. You want to seek the kingdom of God so you can be supplied with what you're missing in the flesh. Praying is essential while fasting because it shows you are doing it for God, not just for self or others. God sees what is done and rewards you accordingly. God is your partner in fasting. God is your adviser in fasting. God is your leader when fasting. You need a leader because you need to know how and when to fast. When you are led by God, you will know exactly when to begin and when to end. Jesus was led to fast by God.

As a matter of fact, as you are fasting you should also indulge yourself in the *scriptures*. Scripture becomes your daily bread and your living water. It is a way for God to feed your spirit and mind at the same time. When your mind and spirit are fed you will feel the presence of the Lord in your life.

It is also good to *meditate* on the word of God as you fast. Meditation is a spiritual sustainer; it will keep you during your fast.

And what good is it to fast without *faith*? Esther, Daniel, Jesus show their faith in God during their fasting. From the moment they step into their fasting until the point God answers their prayers they demonstrate faith. And because of their faith they *gain* victory over the enemy. As you fast, you have to believe that God will supply all your needs.

When you pray you will also learn what kind of fast you ought to engage. Many people have the notion that fasting is only withdrawing from food. They also may think that fasting means not eating anything at all. When you read the scripture, you see that there are different ways to fast, and some may involve withdrawing from food completely and others may involve abstaining from other aspects of life. Yes, food is one way to deny the flesh because it is a common method used by the enemy to strain our relationship with God. To deny food is to break through all the clutter and interferences that clog our relationship with God. Food comes in many forms—from beef to sweets—and if we are serious about fasting, we must sacrifice.

However, there are other interferences based on the culture that must be considered when fasting. As Thoreau suggested, we live in a world that has become a culture of consumption. The constant goods and services, pleasures and distractions of life can block our view of God. When this happens it becomes necessary to look at what we're consuming not only in terms of food but in terms of culture. Are we consuming too much television? Are we consuming too much technology? Are we on the phone, on the Internet, and playing games all day long? If so, we may need to fast in those areas. We may need to sacrifice the technology. We may need to give up television for a week or two. We may need to cut off the phone and the computer for forty days.

Fasting is denying the flesh and the flesh can be tempted in all kinds of ways from tech to sex to money to power; and you may need to sacrifice all these to get closer to God. You have to look to God (pray) and ask Him what is keeping you bound to the enemy and away from God's glory. What is blocking your connection? You have to look at your lifestyle and see if it is pleasing to God. If your lifestyle is displeasing to God, it won't be pleasant for you. You will find yourself striving but never reaching, hoping but never gaining, and breathing but never living. You want to live for God, and the only way to live for God is to fast and pray and remove any malevolence in your way.

Finally, you want to live happy and the only way to live happy is to get rid of anything that may keep you bound and away from God.

# YOU WANT TO BE HAPPY
## (A Song)

*Because I'm happy*
*Clap along if you feel like a room without a roof*
*Because I'm happy*
*Clap along if you feel like happiness is the truth*
*Because I'm happy*
*Clap along if you know what happiness is to you*
*Because I'm happy*
*Clap along if you feel like that's what you wanna do*
    *—Pharrell Williams*

## *James 5:13*

As stated in the introduction, no one wants to live their life being unhappy. The reason for confronting our inadequacies, indecencies, and abnormalities is because we don't want it to be a hindrance to our happiness. I don't know about you, but I don't want to live being unhappy. I want to be happy. I don't want anything or anybody interfering with my peace; and for that reason, I challenge weaknesses and remove discrepancies to live in contentment.

What is advised in this book is easier said than done. I'm not going to feed you the suggestion that all you have to do is have faith and everything will fall into place. While this is true, faith in itself takes work and time to build. I want you to build up your faith. The more you build, the easier life gets and the happier you will be. Faith is a powerful friend and happiness is its cousin. Once you believe, you will receive the joy that comes with *faith, prayer, scripture, meditation, and fasting.*

I think there is a void in many people's lives and that void robs us of happiness. And most people who are unhappy realize it themselves even if they don't admit it to others. People are looking for happiness and realizing that no matter how much money they have or what they do, unless they find the source—the missing particle of their displeasure—there will always be sadness and to a large extent misery in their life. This is no way to live. The sad thing is many people not only live unhappy but die unhappy.

The story of the young rich man in the Bible gives a perfect example of someone who had much and did well but was still unhappy (Matthew 19:16 – 22). Although the story focuses on the young man's quest for eternal life, it also emphasizes the unhappiness he feels in his earthly life—even with all his riches. And it was not his riches that made him unhappy. There was nothing wrong with him being rich. There is nothing wrong with anybody being rich. God is not against being rich and possessing much goods. God blessed Abraham who was rich and his nephew Lot was rich. As a matter of fact, what caused the squabble and the quarrelling between Abraham and Lot was the overabundance of riches and many possessions. The Bible says in Genesis 13 that the land could not support them because of their many possessions and caused infighting between the two camps. However, Abraham decided that he and Lot should separate in order to keep the peace between their two households. Abraham understood that riches and possessions should never be the cause of unhappiness and family disruption.

So as you can see there is nothing wrong with being rich. God can bless the rich like God can bless the poor. In fact Jesus was rich. The Bible says, "For you know the grace of our Lord Jesus Christ, that though he was rich, yet for your sake he became poor, so that you through his poverty might become rich" (2 Corinthians 8:9). As the song goes, "Our Father is rich in houses and land / He holds the power of the world in his hands." Jesus is rich in houses and land but also love and mercy.

The point of this story however, is not about defending or condemning riches, it's about finding the missing link between earthly happiness and eternal life. One should not have to wait until they get to heaven to be happy; that would mean God is limited here on Earth in dealing with our circumstances and emotions. No! God is a God of heaven and Earth and can bless us and make us happy wherever we are. The bible has many verses on happiness. James 5: 13 says, "is anyone happy? Let him sing songs of praise." "Happy is the man that findeth wisdom and the man that geteth understanding" (Proverbs 3:13 KJV). The word blessed is often translated happy: "Blessed is the man that walketh not in the counsel of the ungodly, nor standeth in the way of sinners, nor sitteth in the seat of the scornful. But his delight is in the law of the Lord; and in his law doth he meditate day and night" (Psalm 1:1-2 KJV).

If we read the young rich man's story we will see that having riches and possessing much does not guarantee happiness. There is still something missing in the young rich man's life which is why he seeks out the master for answers.

The young rich man goes to Jesus and asks him, "Teacher, what good thing must I do to get eternal life?" After chastising him on the word good, Jesus tells him, "If you want to enter life, obey the commandments."

"Which ones?" the man inquired.

Jesus says, "Do not murder, do not commit adultery, do not steal, do not bear false witness, honor your father and mother, and 'love your neighbor as yourself.'" The young rich man said emphatically and unequivocally, "All these I have kept."

You would think that a young rich man would have trouble keeping the law. But he was seemingly a descent fella. He was a man concerned with life: He did not kill or murder. He was a man of decency and loyalty—he did not commit adultery. You would think that a young rich man might have a problem in this area. He was a man of honesty—he did not steal to get rich. He was a man of integrity—he did not give false testimony by lying, scheming, or falsely accusing anyone. He was a man with respect for family and community—he honored his father and mother and loved his neighbors. This seemingly good guy has all the attributes of a God-fearing, law-abiding, neighbor-loving man. However, although he had done everything right, he still felt like there was something missing from his life that prevented him from feeling whole, being happy and certain about his home in eternity.

It is surprising when you think about it: You can be a person concerned with humanity, full of integrity, and still be unhappy. You can be a person of honesty and decency and still feel unhappy. You can be a person of loyalty and fidelity and still be unhappy. You can be committed to family and community and still be unhappy.

You can have money, power, and people who love you, and still feel like there is something missing in your life?

"What do I still lack?" is the young rich man's question to Jesus.

Jesus answers, "Go and sell your possessions and give to the poor, and you will have treasures in heaven. Then come, follow me."

According to the scripture: "When the young man heard this, he went away sad, because he had great wealth."

This is truly a sad ending to a great story. But it is also a great lesson on happiness. What the young rich man was missing was sacrifice. The source of his unhappiness was his inability and unwillingness to give up his riches for a greater good and greater life.

Jesus identified what he was "still lacking." He was lacking the ability to actually believe in someone and something other than himself and his riches and he did not have the strength to separate himself from his possessions, give to the poor and follow Jesus. He did not have the desire or the strength to let go of his goods and do a greater good. Instead of giving away all his riches and putting his faith in Jesus, everything he did was for his own good. He was getting rich for himself. He was living a life of integrity for himself, he was being honest for himself, he was loyal to family and community for himself. It was all about him. This was a job without a true connection to God. Therefore, when he was tested, he was unwilling to disconnect himself from himself and from his riches and give it all to others, build up treasures in heaven, and follow Jesus.

If he would have given it all up, it would have showed his trust and faith in God. It would have showed he controlled his riches and his riches didn't control him. It would have further showed he was willing to give it all up for what he desired most—and that was eternal life. Instead the test proved that his riches controlled his life.

Following Jesus would have given him *someone to battle with* against himself and his riches. Connecting with God would have given him *something* (*faith, prayer, scripture, meditation*, and *fasting*) *to battle with* and release him from his selfish ways. When you are doing everything in the name of yourself and not truly for others or God, you can never really be happy in life. You have to let things go that hold you as the enemy's hostage and away from God.

The young rich man had *faith* not in God, but in himself. He *prayed* but only because it was what he was told to do; his heart possibly was not in his prayer. He read the *law* and kept the law, but he never *meditated* on the law day and night. He possibly didn't *fast* because he would have been able to deny the flesh its love and desire for riches and possessions.

When it came time to give up his riches, he showed his true love was his possessions, not eternal life. He only wanted eternal life as part of his possessions. As a result, he walked away sad. "What do you benefit if you gain the whole world but lose your own soul? Is anything worth more than your soul?" (Matthew 16:26 NLT). Apparently keeping riches on Earth was worth more than the man's quest for eternal life. He would rather walk away sad than live happy.

Some people love alcohol and are not willing to give it up for anybody—not their families, not their health, not even God. Some people believe it's all about them: their looks, their life, their possessions; and then wonder why they're not happy and loneliness is their only friend or enemy (depends on how you see it). Some people love food, sex, money, drugs, crime, gambling, stubbornness, selfishness, and other faults more than they do God. They know and they feel that these aberrations are bringing them sadness, but they're unwilling to give them up for others, for God and for true happiness. They know that something is missing in their lives and what's missing is keeping them unhappy, but still they love their obsessions more than they do their happiness. The young rich man, like so many others, would rather settle for temporary satisfaction rather than earthly contentment and eternal life. "He walked away sad."

Jesus wasn't against his riches; Jesus was against his love for riches above love for others and God. The Bible states, "For the love of money is a root of all kinds of evil. Some people, eager for money, have wandered from the faith and pierced themselves with many griefs" (1 Timothy 6:10 NIV). Jesus wasn't trying to hurt him; Jesus was trying to free him, and the only way to free him was to challenge him. Jesus knew he had a lust for possessions and love for riches that surpassed his love for the poor, for earthly happiness and eternal life. Jesus wanted him to challenge himself and free himself from his enemy so that he could build treasures in heaven and live happy on earth. But his weakness pierced his faith and resulted in his grief.

## You must ask yourself two questions:

1)   What am I missing that is keeping me unhappy?
2)   Is there anything I need to give up, to do, to be the happy person that I should be in life?

In order to avoid sadness make sure you have faith in someone other than yourself; God is other than yourself. Make sure you get rid of anything that keeps you bound and controlled and interferes with your love for self, others, and God. Make sure whatever you do is to His glory and then you will truly be happy. You want to be happy in life. "Let your light so shine before men, that they may see your good works, and glorify your father which is in heaven" (Matthew 5:16 KJV). If you're happy and you know it clap your hands! If you're happy and you know it stomp your feet! If you're happy and you know it, and you really want to show it, if you happy and you know it clap your hands! I will "Cause I'm Happy".

# DAILY BATTLE DEVOTION
## (A Piece of Bread and Glass of Water)

*John 6:35*

## *DAY 1*

And the battle is not determined by one's spiritual or secular affiliation, it is determined by one's existence as a part of human creation. Human creation is prone to battles. The first man and woman on Earth had to battle temptation. And the battle was not their choice: the battle was their life. Life brings battles without option and suffering without reason as part of the human experience. So the question is not whether one is going to have battles, the question is whether one is going to succumb or confront their battles. To succumb is to give in, submit, surrender. To confront is to oppose, challenge, resist. Some people will not battle against temptation; they will surrender to their personal weaknesses. Yet, there are those who will contend with temptation. They will fight when they realize temptation is ruining their lives, disrupting their families, and causing serious unhappiness.
p 9

## DAY 2

Some people love alcohol and are not willing to give it up for anybody—not their families, not their health, not even God. Some people believe it's all about them: their looks, their life, their possessions; and then wonder why they're not happy and loneliness is their only friend or enemy (depends on how you see it). Some people love food, sex, money, drugs, crime, gambling, stubbornness, selfishness, and other faults more than they do God. They know and they feel that these aberrations are bringing them sadness, but they're unwilling to give them up for others, for God and for true happiness. They know that something is missing in their lives and what's missing is keeping them unhappy, but still they love their obsessions more than they do their happiness. The young rich man, like so many others, would rather settle for temporary satisfaction rather than earthly contentment and eternal life. "He walked away sad." p 85

## DAY 3

If you deal with the issue without God you will lose the battle. The enemy would love for you to go into battle without God. Some people move so impetuously. When you go into battle without God the flesh begins to say things to escalate the problem rather than defuse it. You have to remember: Flesh responds evil for evil and insult for insult. You need fasting to keep the flesh in check so that it does not resort to evil. When you fast and pray you are asking God to control your actions and monitor your speech. You don't need to respond to everything thrown at you from the enemy; that just shows a lack of faith. p 71

## DAY 4

The enemy would love for you to desecrate and disrespect your body because it opens the door to disease and damnation. You want to do all you can to protect your body, and the best way to protect the body is to fast and pray. Fasting keeps the body regal and the face glowing with God's glory. When you glow with the glory of God you can rely on your own compliments. You can tell yourself you look good. You don't need compliments from anyone else to feel good because the glow of God speaks for itself. Some folks are always waiting on other people's praises, but when you have fasted and prayed God has already spoken to you about yourself and you should know how good you look because God is good.  p 73

## DAY 5

We have all fallen short of the glory of God and temptation is the reason we have fallen. However, temptation also causes us to fall short in life. Falling short in life is submitting to influences that control our being. Those influences can be internal—such as fear, jealousy, and insecurity, as well as external—such as alcohol, food, and money. One can be tempted to give in to sickness, to accept weakness, and to partake in laziness. One can be tempted to holler, hit, kick, spit, and slap. Temptation induces a host of people, feelings, and actions. When we fall short in life, we also fall short of God's glory for our lives.  p 15

## DAY 6

The flesh can be easily manipulated by powerful agents of captivity, from food to clothes to shopping to technology to sex and so much more that it's hard to see God in the crowd. It's hard to hear God in the noise. It's hard to find God when you're lost in the world. The enemy puts up such a buffer between us and God that it's going to take a miracle to tear down the walls and get closer to God. When you fast you tear down walls that separate you from God. When you fast you get less static and better communication with God. Fasting breaks down the buffer and removes the interruption of the world that blocks our connection with God.  p 69

## DAY 7

You need faith to battle temptation. Faith is the ability to believe in someone other than yourself. God is other than yourself. What makes God other than yourself is that God is much bigger, better, and stronger than you. God is omnipotent, omniscient, and omnipresent. There is no one in existence like or even close to being like God. And if you're going to battle temptation you need someone much bigger, better, and stronger than you. Temptation is strong and you alone do not have the ability or strength to take on the enemy; if you did you wouldn't keep falling to temptation.     p 19

## DAY 8

The self alone is prone to weakness, sickness, and sadness, and there-fore can be unreliable and limited in its ability to fight temptation. The enemy wants you to believe *only* in yourself because he knows you alone cannot beat temptation and he cannot beat God. The enemy will keep you from God to take advantage of your life. When the enemy takes control of your life he uses you for his own pleasure and then dumps you on the road of self-destruction. In order to avoid self-destruction you need to put your faith in someone other than yourself. When you put your faith in God you get the power needed to take on temptation. You get the knowledge needed to outsmart the enemy and you get a God that will never leave you or forsake you in battle. p 19

## DAY 9

But the flesh is often used as the antithesis of God's purpose. The spirit is willing but the flesh is weak. Weak flesh causes havoc in our lives. Weak flesh increases the enemy's ability to lure the body into temptation. The body seeks satisfaction and overindulgence in its greed. The body wants glamour, pleasure, fame, and an abundance of food. Satisfying the flesh can get you into a lot of trouble. The enemy knows what the body wants and will provide all the desires to keep flesh under control. When you are under the enemy's control you are constantly sinning against God. The enemy will use your flesh to keep you away from God because the enemy knows that if you reach God, God will save you from the flesh. When the enemy lures your body he puts you at odds with God's spiritual purpose for your life. When the spirit and flesh are at odds, a battle rages inside you. In order for the spirit of God to win the battle you need something to go into battle with and the best weapon to take into battle is fasting.   p 68

## DAY 10

Faith is *practical*: It will take you into battle even when you're doubtful. You can use faith to battle evil. Faith is what you use when you're going into battle. You don't go into battle empty-handed. Faith arms you for battle. It is a real weapon in battle against disbelief. And you're going to need to battle disbelief if you're going to fight the whole battle. Some people believe at first, like Peter, and then half way through the battle they lose faith. True faith keeps you fighting to the finish. With faith you can face life and face death. With faith you can fight for life and fight against death. Many people are afraid of death but faith conquers death like faith conquers life. Faith keeps you fighting to the very last breath.      p 21

## DAY 11

Even when you fall you must believe you will win. Falling is not the end but rather part of the process towards the victory. All things work for the good, including the fall, when you're with God in battle. Everyone falls in life but not everyone gets up. Faith keeps you believing even when you've fallen. As a matter of fact the only way to get back up is by faith. Faith picks you up when you're down. Faith is your legs, your arms, your courage. Without faith you would stay down, cry in your pain, and wallow in your shame. But with faith you get up with your tears, fight the power in spite of your pain and run on regardless of your disgrace. Faith keeps you getting up every time you fall. Remember faith is for real. It provides the necessary substance needed for your restoration.    p 21

## DAY 12

Neither you nor anyone like you can battle alone against temptation and win. As you know people can be unpredictable and unreliable. They can be with you one minute and against you the next. They can be on your side in one battle and nowhere to be found the next round. The enemy can even use friends and family to tempt you rather than help you in battle. The enemy is shrewd, but God is faithful. When you put your faith in God there is a guarantee that God will always be with you; that God will never go up against you and God will never turn his back on you. God is with you in good times and in bad times, in sickness and in health, in poverty and in riches, in freedom and in prison. God is faithful. p 22

## DAY 13

When you feel like your faith is running out, you need to ask God to increase your faith. God can increase faith. God can increase your faith to help you go further in your battle. When you receive increased faith it gives you more patience to wait for the Lord, more truth to trust in God, and more courage to resist temptation. The truth is, at times you will be in your mess longer than you expect, and it will seem as if God is deaf and the enemy is all that's left. But faith is able to extend beyond the length of your suffering. Faith knows how to wait on God. When you are able to go the distance with God, it not only shows that God is with you but that you are with God. And in order to be with God you must have faith.　　p 23

## DAY 14

The feeling of confidence and reassurance as a result of faith will lead you to challenge things and do the things you once feared. The enemy uses fear to inhibit our progress and prevent our success. *Many people* have missed out on dreams and goals because of fear. Many people are too afraid to step outside their homes, step outside their community, step outside their culture—all because of fear. Fear is a great source of regret and frustration in many people's lives. And it is a shame when someone misses out on life and all the blessings that God has for them because they cower in fear. However, when you have God on your side you walk by faith and not by fear.  p 24

## DAY 15

*Many people* will not step out on faith but will be kicked out by force. Don't get mad, this may be God's plan for your life. God may need to kick you out of your current job, marriage or home so that you can learn to walk by faith. Some people will never become the person that they ought to be until they get kicked out of their comfort zone. You will never get out of where you are and get to where God wants you to be if you don't get pushed out. However, the brutal is not always that bad. All things work for the good of those that love the Lord. The good thing about God is that even when you get kicked out, you still land on faith. When Peter fell in the water Jesus caught him. God will catch you whether you step out or get kicked out and it's up to you to learn to walk by faith whichever way you come out.　　p 26

## DAY 16

And there is no doubt you will get wounded and scarred in battle against the enemy. Cancer can wound and scar you mentally, physically and spiritually. Your scars will be seen on your body, by the loss of your hair and by the dysfunction of some of your faculties. However, it's better to come through the battle wounded than to not come through the battle at all. Your wounds show that you put up a good fight and that the enemy couldn't take you down easily. You didn't give into sorrow. You didn't allow pain and weakness to have the final word. You didn't allow physical changes to your body to steal your fight for life and living. You fought the good fight.  p 26

## DAY 17

You can actually walk through suffering with faith. Whether you're suffering because of loss or because of consequences it can be exhausting spiritually, physically and emotionally. It can rob you of all the strength you have in the bank of divinity. Many people have actually begun to believe in their suffering over their faith in God. To believe in suffering is to submit to its powers and surrender to its sorrows. However, while suffering is draining faith is enabling. Faith keeps you believing there is a way out of suffering to a greater hope and happiness. While suffering is paralyzing faith is energizing. Faith actually picks you up and pushes you on, up and out of darkness. Faith keeps the lamp on. Faith actually gives you light to see better, comfort to feel better and hope to think better. The best counter punch to suffering is faith. p 27

## DAY 18

You need prayer to battle temptation. Prayer is communing with someone other than yourself. The reason why you need to commune with someone other than yourself is because temptation talks to you. Temptation tells you what to do. Temptation is a feeling against your will and a thought against your thinking. It tells you to do things you should not do and blocks any communication that may free you. Many people submit to temptation because that's the only voice they hear. And when that's the only voice you hear, that's the only voice you follow. Prayer gives an alternative voice to temptation. Prayer gives you an opportunity to go outside of yourself and speak to God. When you speak to God, you set up a face-to-face battle between God and temptation. In fact, the best time to pray is when you are face to face with temptation. As soon as you feel temptation coming on, pray.   p 29

## DAY 19

Prayer calls attention to your weakness and cries to God for *resistance*. The more you recognize your weakness, the more you pray against it, the more you can resist it. Resisting temptation is the greatest conversation you can have with God because it relieves you of any pain and suffering that come with transgression. If you can resist temptation, you don't have to worry about the consequences of your actions. No fall, no bad consequence. It is great when you can walk away, run away, or shout down your temptation because it gives you control over your actions and when you have control over your actions you live happier.   p 31

## DAY 20

But the strongest prayer is when you can talk to God about light in the midst of darkness, hope in the midst of despair, and strength in the midst of brokenness. Yes, you may be in a permanent state of loss as a result of your fall, but that does not mean your situation should destroy your life. You can still live. As long as you have breath, you can talk to God. Talk to God about how to live in your new state. The greatest battle comes when you can talk to God about finding *happiness* in the midst of sadness. Many people are living happy lives with disease, after divorce or life imprisonment. They've learned to live with God rather than live with fault, and when you live with

God you see things differently. You don't need to look at life through the lens of your suffering, you can look at it from the perspective of God's promise to always be present, no matter what happens. While the enemy puts your mind on the worse of your condition, God turns your eyes to the work of his perfection. God can still use you and renew you for his wonder.  p 33

## DAY 21

If you don't care if you live or die you have lost all meaning in life; you have discarded what is sacred. When you discard what is sacred you discard God, who gave you life. Your life is to be cherished and used for God's purpose, whatever state you find yourself in. But the enemy can make you believe your life is worthless. When you believe your life is worthless you have no problem committing suicide, or drinking yourself to death, or doing something careless to wreck your life. The enemy loves it when people go down this road because it shows they have neither the light of God to guide them nor the presence of God to keep them. This is the enemy's best time to tempt, but it's also God's best time to work. Believe it or not this is where God operates best, if you just look to God for a moment. If you find the energy to mumble out a little prayer of faith, you will see God is able to restore you to your senses. You will see that God is with you in your crisis. God will show you His glory and mercy. God's grace will step in and pull you out of foolish thinking and return you to wisdom. God's mercy will bring you from worthlessness to worthiness. God's love will rescue you from sin and suicidal thinking and place you on a rock of revival. All it takes is one *faithful* prayer, which God will give you to save yourself.  p 34

## DAY 22

Remember, you don't know what can happen in a day. You don't know what temptation has planned for you. Before you woke up, the enemy was already up planning your fall. You want to pray before you step out the door. You want to walk out ready for battle. Prayer gets you ready for battle. Pray for patience. Pray for silence. Pray for understanding. Pray for wisdom. Prayerful preparation helps you prior to temptation. The patience will help you with anger. The silence will help you with conversation. The understanding will help you with imbeciles and the wisdom will help you with decisions.  p 36

## DAY 23

Don't underestimate prayer as a potent force to be used in any and every situation. While you're praying, you're talking to God, and you're releasing your stress and anger and any discomfort you may have with life. Some people go crazy because they have no one to talk to. Many people find themselves breaking down and crying to themselves every night. Life can be so exasperating and exhausting, so unfair and cruel, but God is *so* good. God opens his ear to every care we have and every word we speak. Everybody needs somebody to talk to; thank God we can *take it to the Lord in prayer*. We can take our frustrations, annoyances and dilemmas to God. God allows us to share every temperament with Him. Every attitude He accepts. When you talk to God and confess your sins you don't have to worry about God spreading your business to anyone. God is a safe keeper; you can trust God with all your information.      p 37

## DAY 24

You need scripture to battle temptation. Scripture is the written word of God. It contains information, inspiration, and instructions beyond what you already have to support your fight. If you are going to battle temptation you need words that will inform you, inspire you, and instruct you in life. The enemy's words are full of misinformation, disempowerment, and misdirection, which all will only lead to your destruction. If you're going to battle the enemy you need words beyond the enemy's words. You need the word of God. When you get the word of God it battles the enemy's words and builds up resistance to temptation.  p 39

## DAY 25

Some people are so easily tempted by anything. They will eat anything, sleep with anything, drink anything, get angry over anything,
can't wait for anything, and don't listen to anything. When you are
so easily tempted by anything, it is a serious problem that the enemy
enjoys but God abhors. God does not like to see his people suffer so
God contends with the enemy through his word. God gives people
the sword, which is the word of God, so that they can cut down anything coming at them. This is a real battle. When you are able to cut
down anything you are also able to cut down suffering in your life.
When you cut down suffering you cut down the chains that bind you
and free yourself from temptation's control. When you free yourself
from temptation's control you are no longer identified with your past
mistakes rather you are aligned with your present success.  p 40

## DAY 26

According to the scripture, if you have been set free, you are free
indeed. "So if the Son sets you free, you will be free indeed" (John 8:36
NIV). When you are free indeed you don't identify yourself with your
failure, you identify yourself with your freedom. *Free indeed* erases
your past so you can live in your present and move towards a greater
future. Your latter life in God will be better than your former life in
sin. You are a conqueror, an overcomer, a survivor, a valiant soldier.
Words are significant, and how you describe yourself is important to
your future aspirations and connections. You are connected to God
and God is power. The word of God gives you information which
tells you that you are more than a conqueror. "In all these things we
are more than conquerors through him that loved us" (Romans 8:37
KJV). When you are a conqueror you have crushed your addiction
into oblivion and are no longer associated with its remnants. When
you are a conqueror you feel confident and secure in yourself as a

person. God's word has a way of boosting your self-esteem and worth. God's word makes you feel like somebody, and the better you feel the better you fight.  p 41

## DAY 27

The word of God prepares you for the reality of life. Many people are fooled into believing because they serve God they will have no problems. This is not the reality. How do you prove God is real if you have no problems? If you read the scriptures you will see that God's servants had enemies. God's servants had disappointments. God's servants failed and sinned and cried and bled. When you study the word of God you will realize that walking with Him is not easy. It can be difficult and tumultuous, slippery and dangerous. When some people find out they face the same troubles with God as without God, maybe even more difficulties with God than without God, they decide to leave God. But God's word never said you would have no troubles, God's word says He will never leave you alone in trouble. "I will never leave you nor forsake you" (Joshua 1:5 NIV).  p 45

## DAY 28

You need meditation in battle. Meditation is the ability to go beyond yourself and into your spirit. Your mind, body, and soul are often used by the enemy to do his bidding; however, when you meditate on God you go deep into your spirit, where you can speak to God and God can speak to you. Meditation helps you to lose yourself in God. You want to lose yourself in God. When you lose yourself in God, you find yourself in God's Spirit. You want to find yourself in the Holy Spirit. Meditation is the ability to absorb God and all his perfection into your own spirit so that every aspect of God becomes part of your living. To have God in your spirit is to reflect God's goodness in your life. God's goodness is His love, grace, mercy, peace, patience, joy, and forgiveness.  p 51

## DAY 29

Meditation is a deep concentration that shifts your attention from your suffering to your overcoming. Many people suffer from anxiety, stress, and trauma, and these aberrations can cause serious unhappiness in life. The enemy loves that lives are disrupted and distracted because of abnormalities; however, meditation digs into your spirit to pull out peace and happiness to confront disturbances and shift your attention. With meditation, you focus on peace to replace anxiety and stress and you concentrate on joy to subdue and control trauma. Meditation makes you think of peaceful people, places, and times that bring happiness to your life. Meditation brings calm and control to your existence. Meditation is like medicine; it gets into your spirit to heal your mind, body, and soul. It releases you from any abnormalities so you can focus on God's glory, beauty, and wonder in your life. When David's soul was troubled he sought the beauty of the Lord, "One thing have I desired of the Lord, that will I seek after; that I may dwell in the house of the Lord all the days of my life, *to behold the beauty* of the Lord, and to enquire in his temple" (Psalm 27:4 KJV). p 52

## DAY 30

I understand that some people may not love themselves because of what other people have said and done. You may not love yourself because other people have been mean and cruel in their wording and in their treatment of you. You may have been called really bad and disgusting names by other people—stupid, dumb, no good, lazy, ugly, et cetera. You may even believe the names you've been called. You may have been treated horribly by other people—been sexually abused, violated, molested, cheated on, lied to, physically abused, abandoned, et cetera. This may have wrecked your life and caused you to do things that are dirty, disgusting, and wrong. But this is where you must meditate on God's goodness. You must go into battle against every wrong that you've been called and encountered with the goodness of God.

God's goodness can beat down all the badness that has been done to you. Start by listing each wrong in your life that holds you hostage and then counter it with God's love to keep you, God's power to free you, God's beauty to hold you and God's protection to bring you through it all. Then leave all the wrong behind, shut the door and walk in the spirit and the freedom of God's Goodness. God's goodness can free you from all the filth you've been called and cleanse you from all the wrongs you've endured.   p 61

## DAY 31

Your new lifestyle will automatically align you with new people and disengage you from old friends. Some people you will leave and other people will leave you. The transition won't be easy but it will be worth it. Whatever you do, don't turn back. Keep going with the flow of your fast. It will take you through sickness and sadness to lead you to safety and happiness. You will go through the valley, lose friends and family but become a better person that attracts a different standard and quality of people. After a while the old life will be a distant memory and the new life will be a great reality. As with Jesus, you will become more powerful and knowledgeable after a forty day fast. Every day of the fast you will get stronger and smarter. Every day of the fast you build up resistance and determination to go all the way. Even if you fall, you get up and walk on. Every day of the fast you will become a better person. You want to be a better person. You want to be a humble person. You want to be a kind person. You want to be considerate and self-controlled. When you are new and better, you will attract new and better people. Whatever you are is what you will attract; *you reap what you sow.*   p 76

# INDEX

www.ingramcontent.com/pod-product-compliance
Lightning Source LLC
Chambersburg PA
CBHW071059090426
42737CB00013B/2391